From Poráč to Pennsylvania

Pisani list na 9ho oktora 1935
Yungston Oh

Slava i Jezukristu milo asumno pozdravina
naj vampervse ot miloho panaboha atak ot mariji
Civilla Da amojej fameliji ato pretebe katko i mar
 x cina tak x vas bars krasni pozdravujem onoja
luba sestro katko i tvoho chlopa tati pisem želem
nebar ziZrava bolem slabx tajin sohoze rovaja vam
vincujem apismolem Jostala i tal pi cer vizevas tlus
ta i marcin ere stemolate ati pisem želem i hanino pis
moja citala asimi pisala u shlopom pipsebuti cipoes
hlopa jamala i persoho Dobrono i Vrukoho tanise
cne bolem teras Dama Deseskvatim tasama choetju
ka primi ta onazloynom amazk ite kubajsam ajaxe
dama lakebi stal tabim mustovas i palenki kupila
atak i tem racintir chockeli akohit alem mikupila
komen taki coto i pre meme polovi ca joho apolovi
ca moja toveliki stoji tri sta tatari laitem chockle
ti opačiti totmuj Dum ati pisem sestro katko žea
mebuli obifvi phanom unevjorka navekesin
uagusti zatvalizni umojej Žofki i vmajka iZes
Zotum i zuska moji stivi lam bivaju tazmecho
Zili kolo tej voti velikej zeme sebuli kupati
čo semuji vesti nasiji trikotini toZaleko otnevjorka
hanasebars bajala jajij hvarila žebisme isli Jokraja
tanevbtila anasami Jen matki božej uspenije včar
osetem hotin zmeisli Jonevjorka nasa tazmetam
buli Jatvanac naji vaksi so apolyum navesterant
tomas vzal hanin kurier vun donej skvaju prisole

From Poráč to Pennsylvania

Reflections
of
Mária Ďurica Širila Ďurša

(Her Life and Times in Slovakia, Pennsylvania, and Ohio)

SHARON ZIRBES FULLER

For
JUSTINA, MY MOTHER
(Na pamiatku, in memory)

And for her grandchildren:
PHOEBE AND **JOHN**

And for her great grandchildren:
LIAM, DAVID, BODINE, KEENAN, HATTIE

The persons who showed me Spiš and Poráč journey now by another path, and so this history is dedicated to my uncle and my cousin:

Michael Sirilla (1898-1995) of Perryopolis, PA and **Štefan Cvengroš (1922-2002)** of Rudňany, Slovakia.

October 6, 1986, Perryopolis, PA   Author's photo.

"Keep memory alive; if we forget, we are guilty." Elie Wiesel, 1984.

Contents

We who write about the past were not there.

We can never be certain that we have recaptured it

as it really was. But the least we can do is

stay within the evidence....

The trick is selecting the right, true, details,

and using them in the right place.

--Barbara Tuchman

from Practicing History: Selected Essays, 1982.

To know who you are you have to know where your story began.

From the book Poráč by Š. Hanuščin, 2003, p.4.

A-Z maps online. Slovakia in the heart of Europe.

A-Z maps online. Villuge of Poráč.

Preface

Let's start with the very beginning of my interest in immigration. Every summer during my early childhood and early teen years (1940s-1950s), my parents, my sister, and I traveled from our home in Tinley Park, IL by car to Youngstown, OH to visit my mother's mother, Mary Dursa, my grandmother, at her home at 722 Steel Street. I knew she was "foreign" because instead of a big hug and "Hello, how are you?" she would say, *"Dobrý deň,"* and *"Jak sa maš?"* For me, my sister, and my confused father, who was of German heritage, this was the way every visit started and usually every visit ended with *"gutbye,"* her version of *"goodbye."* None of my schoolmates ever talked about a "foreign" grandmother needless to say one who came from nowhere, somewhere far, far away in a place called Slovakia in a country that was once called Czechoslovakia. Many years later, I was to read the English translation of the Czech novel *Babička (Granny)* by the noted Czech writer Božena Němcová, and I knew then that the language and cultural barriers of my grandmother's "foreign" origin were brick walls that could never be scaled between me and her. As a 3rd generation American child, I was embarrassed, disinterested, and saddened by these annual visits to Youngstown. At this time it was not popular to talk about one's foreign heritage. It wasn't until the '70s that admitting one's "ethnicity" evolved.

Time heals. Grandma died on July 3, 1955, and as I stared at her image from the coffin placed in her own living room and saw the amount of family and friends who came to pay their last respects, I felt regret: how sad that I never captured the real person behind that Slovak woman. She emigrated, leaving her parents in the Slovak village, adjusted to the life of a wife of a coal miner in Fayette County, Pennsylvania, bearing 10 children between the years 1891 and 1907 and being widowed in 1908 with 7 dependent children. She cared for boarders to have additional income, remarried in 1910 and bore 2 more children while raising an orphaned nephew. She was widowed again in 1934, and left, as part of her estate in 1955, two houses, paid for, on Steel Street in Youngstown, and 32 grandchildren. What ambition. What tenacity. What dreams. What "grit" we would say today. This was a *strong* woman.

In the fall of 1957, while a senior at the University of Illinois, Urbana campus, with an English/history major, I enrolled in a course called "The History of Immigration." The reading list for this course included some classics like Oscar Handlin's *The Uprooted* (1951); Carl Wittke's *We Who Built America* (1939); Thomas Bell's *Out of this Furnace* (1941); Willa Cather's *My Antonia* (1918). The final project for this course was to compile a history of a family immigrant and his/her descendants, ending with myself. This family history was to be based on an interview with a living person in the family tree, using not just birth, marriage, and death data, but physical and personal traits of the émigré. For information on my maternal Slovak grandmother, I interviewed my aunt, Helen Kostelnik, a resident of Chicago at the time. Much of the information she gave me was "almost the truth," (I later discovered) because she, like many 2nd generation Americans, emphasized melting into the American English language and culture, and making something of yourself meant making money. And she did just that.

Many years later, (1984 to present) with time, internet sources, and 11 visits already to the ancestral Slovak village of Poráč, the incentive to tell my grandmother's story became imminent. (Lisa Alzo's publication in 2004 of *Three Slovak Women* was also an impetus.) My grandmother was no daughter of a count or noble, no wife of a rich man, and she had no education beyond the 5th grade, but she survived as an immigrant woman in a new country.

This is her story, divided into five parts: **Introduction:** Death of husband; **Part One:** Her return to Poráč, Slovakia; **Part Two:** Her return to Pennsylvania (Fayette County); **Part Three:** Her move to

Youngstown, Ohio. **Part Four:** Her death and Epilogue. The Appendix includes the Acknowledgments and End Notes which give factual information about the letters.

Mária's story is told through her (1) letters (based on fact) written from Poráč to her sister Anna in the US, as a new widow with 5 dependent children with her, and (2) letters (based on fact) written from Pennslyvania and Ohio to her sister Katarína (Katka) in Rudňany, Slovakia.   (Katka was the only sibling to stay in Europe.) The two _original_ letters of Mária's, written to her sister Katka from Youngstown, were found in the "shoebox" of my cousin Štefan Cvengroš in Rudňany, Slovakia in 1984 and copied for me. These were written to Katka (his grandmother) in the Spiš dialect and brought home by me and later translated into English. Copies of these two letters are included, as are two _original_ letters written to Mária's daughter, my mother, Justina (Esther) in Tinley Park, IL before both of their deaths. All other letters are based on genealogical research and stories told by family members.

This work was inspired by truth (documents) but was invariably embellished with imagination based on family stories handed down. It's inevitable when recording the past that nonfiction can cross over into fiction and become narrative nonfiction.   Hopefully the reader will feel the integrity of the story, whether documented or embellished. The Endnotes give supplemental facts for most of the letters.

Helpful Hints:
1.   **Acknowledgments** are summarized at the beginning of the End Notes in the Appendix.
2.   The states' names are signified with the current acronyms: PA, OH, NY, etc.
3.   Slovak surnames are spelled as they are spelled today in Slovakia. ie: Ďurica; Širila; Ďurša. Exceptions are the changes in spellings made by families after emigration to the US: Dyuritza; Duritsa; Duritza; Dorris; Sirilla; Shirilla; Shrilla, etc.
     Hungarian spellings are prevalent on internet sources prior to 1918.
4.   The use of Slovak language sayings and Mária's conversations in Slovak have been written in today's standard Slovak, based on the speech of central Slovakia. Proof reading of the Slovak language was made by Lenka Kmaková, a Slovak native speaker. To be true to the language spoken by Mária during her lifetime would necessitate using the Spiš dialect, which is seen in the copies of her original letters.
5.   A detailed Slovak language pronunciation guide is part of the Appendix. Here are a few helpful guides to pronunciation of Slovak language used in this story:
     1.   A mark called an **"acute"** (a dash over a vowel) makes the vowel sound long
          á = Mária pronounced Mahria with the accent on the first syllable
          Í = Katarína, pronounced Katareena, accent on the first syllable
     2.   A mark called a **"háčik"** (a small "v" above a letter) gives the letter a soft sound
          č = Poráč pronounced Porach
          Š = Širila pronounced Shirila
          ň = Rudňany pronounced Rudnynee
     3.   The letter "c" in Slovak is pronounced "ts" or "tz" so "Ďurica" is pronounced Djuritza.

For more information from additional documents used as reference in this memoir, see the
Sirila Tree on www.ancestry.com Most public libraries subscribe to this website. Ask the reference department at your local library to help you access this tree.

Sharon Zirbes Fuller, December, 2018, Steamboat Springs, CO

Ancestors of Maria Durica

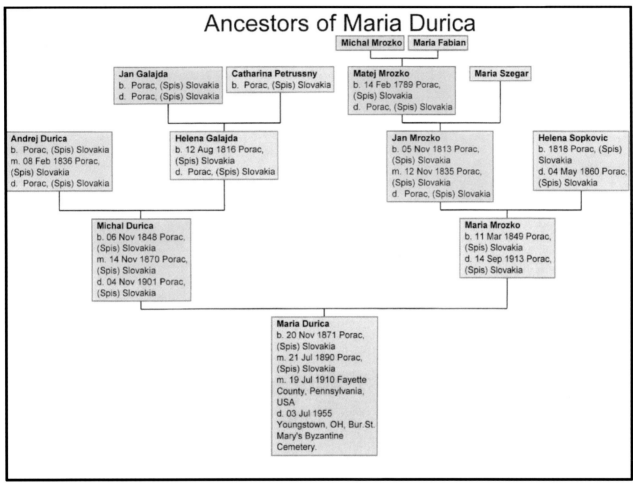

Michal Mrozko	**Maria Fabian**

Jan Galajda
b. Porac, (Spis) Slovakia
d. Porac, (Spis) Slovakia

Catharina Petrussny
b. Porac, (Spis) Slovakia

Matej Mrozko
b. 14 Feb 1789 Porac, (Spis) Slovakia
d. Porac, (Spis) Slovakia

Maria Szegar

Andrej Durica
b. Porac, (Spis) Slovakia
m. 08 Feb 1836 Porac, (Spis) Slovakia
d. Porac, (Spis) Slovakia

Helena Galajda
b. 12 Aug 1816 Porac, (Spis) Slovakia
d. Porac, (Spis) Slovakia

Jan Mrozko
b. 05 Nov 1813 Porac, (Spis) Slovakia
m. 12 Nov 1835 Porac, (Spis) Slovakia
d. Porac, (Spis) Slovakia

Helena Sopkovic
b. 1818 Porac, (Spis) Slovakia
d. 04 May 1860 Porac, (Spis) Slovakia

Michal Durica
b. 06 Nov 1848 Porac, (Spis) Slovakia
m. 14 Nov 1870 Porac, (Spis) Slovakia
d. 04 Nov 1901 Porac, (Spis) Slovakia

Maria Mrozko
b. 11 Mar 1849 Porac, (Spis) Slovakia
d. 14 Sep 1913 Porac, (Spis) Slovakia

Maria Durica
b. 20 Nov 1871 Porac, (Spis) Slovakia
m. 21 Jul 1890 Porac, (Spis) Slovakia
m. 19 Jul 1910 Fayette County, Pennsylvania, USA
d. 03 Jul 1955 Youngstown, OH, Bur.St. Mary's Byzantine Cemetery.

b: birth   m: marriage   d: death

Children of Mária Ďurica Širila Ďurša (Author's archive.)

Mary, 1891-1918   **Katie**, 1892-1956   **Sophie**, 1897-1967   **Mike**, 1898-1995

 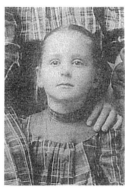  

Joe, 1900-1973   **Anna**, 1902-1918   **Helen**, 1903-2002   **Esther**, 1905-1954

Nicholas, 1906-1907   **Sue**, 1907-1995   **Vera**, 1911-2001   **Julia**, 1913-1998

Family Group Sheet for Maria Durica

Husband:	Michal Sirila	

Birth:	12 Oct 1867 in Porac, (Spis) Slovakia
Death:	02 Nov 1908 in Lemont, Fayette, PA Bur. St Stephen's Greek Catholic Cemetery
Marriage:	21 Jul 1890 in Porac (Spis) Slovakia
Father:	Juraj Sirila
Mother:	Maria Cvengros

Wife:	Maria Durica

Birth:	20 Nov 1871 in Porac, (Spis) Slovakia
Death:	03 Jul 1955 in Youngstown, OH Bur. St Mary's Byzantine Cemetery
Father:	Michael Durica
Mother:	Maria Mrozko
Other Spouses:	Michael Dursa (19 Jul 1910 in New Salem, Fayette, PA)

Children:

**1
F**

Name:	Maria Sirilla
Birth:	22 May 1891 in Porac, (Spis) Slovakia
Death:	11 Nov 1918 in Dawson, Fayette, PA Bur. St Stephen's Greek Catholic Cemetery
Marriage:	30 Jul 1906 in Uniontown, Fayette, PA
Spouse:	John Novak

**2
F**

Name:	Katharine Sirilla
Birth:	08 Sep 1892 in Porac, (Spis) Slovakia
Death:	26 Jan 1956 in Uniontown, Fayette, PA Bur. Hopwood Cemetery, Uniontown
Marriage:	14 Sep 1908 in Leisenring, Fayette, PA
Spouse:	John Duritsa
Other Spouses:	Anton Kalich

**3
F**

Name:	Sophie Sirilla
Birth:	07 Mar 1897 in Hubbard, Trumbull, OH
Death:	17 Jan 1967 in Yonkers, Westchester, NY Bur. St Joseph's Cemetery, Yonkers
Marriage:	25 Nov 1915
Spouse:	Andrew Kuchta

**4
M**

Name:	Michael Sirilla
Birth:	06 Oct 1898 in Lemont Furnace, Fayette, PA
Death:	27 Apr 1995 in Perryopolis, Fayette, PA Bur. St Stephen's Byzantine Cemetery
Marriage:	20 Oct 1923 in Perryopolis, Fayette, PA St Nicholas Greek Catholic Church
Spouse:	Helen Sohanage

**5
M**

Name:	Joseph Sirilla
Birth:	02 Mar 1900 in Lemont Furnace, Fayette, PA
Death:	25 Jan 1973 in Youngstown, Mahoning, OH Bur. Calvary Cemetery
Marriage:	24 Jun 1925 in Perryopolis, Fayette, PA St Nicholas Greek Catholic Church
Spouse:	Catherine Dzurilla

**6
F**

Name:	Anna Sirilla
Birth:	01 Jan 1902 in Lemont Furnace, Fayette, PA
Death:	21 Nov 1918 in North Union, Fayette, PA Bur. Hopwood Cemetery, Uniontown
Spouse:	Stephen Odiske

Family Group Sheet for Maria Durica

7 F	Name: Birth: Death: Marriage: Spouse: Other Spouses:	Helen Sirilla 16 Jul 1903 in Lemont Furnace, Fayette, PA 12 Feb 2002 in Hollywood, CA Bur. Holy Cross Catholic Cemetery 1919 in Perryopolis, Fayette, PA St Nicholas Greek Catholic Church Alex Conrad Peter A. Kostelnik
8 F	Name: Birth: Death: Marriage: Spouse:	Esther Justina Sirilla 16 Mar 1905 in Lemont Furnace, Fayette, PA 21 Aug 1954 in Hazelcrest, Cook, IL Bur. Holy Sepulcher Cemetery, Worth, IL 07 Oct 1934 in Crown Point, Lake, IN George Peter Zirbes
9 M	Name: Birth: Death:	Nicholas Sirilla 15 Nov 1906 in Lemont Furnace, Fayette, PA 18 Jan 1907 in Lemont, Fayette, PA Bur. St Stephen's Greek Catholic Cemetery
10 F	Name: Birth: Death:	Susanna Sirilla 14 Dec 1907 in Lemont Furnace, Fayette, PA 29 Mar 1995 in St Petersburg, Pinellas, FL
11 F	Name: Birth: Death: Marriage: Spouse:	Veronica Dursa 28 May 1911 in Lemont Furnace, Fayette, PA 26 Apr 2001 in Youngstown, Mahoning, OH Bur. Tod Cemetery 30 Sep 1932 in Youngstown, Mahoning, OH John Mathew (Dutch) Pallo
12 F	Name: Birth: Death: Marriage: Spouse:	Julia Dursa 13 Apr 1913 in Vanderbilt, Fayette, PA 07 Sep 1998 in Youngstown, Mahoning, OH Bur. Calvary Cemetery 28 Nov 1931 in Youngstown, Mahoning, OH John Lesnak

Family Group Sheet for Michael Dursa

Husband:	Michael Dursa
Birth: Death: Father: Mother: Other Spouses:	05 Nov 1872 in Porac, (Spis) Slovakia 23 Oct 1934 in Youngstown, Mahoning, OH Bur. St Mary's Greek Catholic Cemetery John Dursa Anna Polkabla Maria Durica (19 Jul 1910 in New Salem, Fayette, PA)

Wife:	Maria Dursa
Birth: Death: Father: Mother:	Slovakia Feb 1907 Unknown Unknown

Children:	
1 M	Name: Birth: Death:	Steve Dursa 31 Aug 1902 in Fayette County, PA 16 Jun 1920 in Star Junction, Fayette, PA

INTRODUCTION

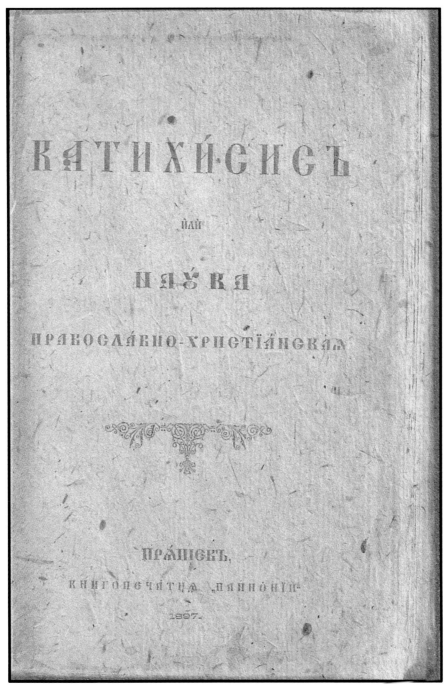

Cover of Michael Sirilla's (Maria's husband) catechism booklet of the Greek Catholic Church, written in Old Slavonic, published by Pannonia Publishers, 1897. Author's archive.

Levoča 22. 7. 1987

Birth Certificate | V Ý P I S

z matriky — ~~úradného druhopisu matriky~~ pokrstených farského úradu cirkvi

gr. kat. fary   v   Poráči   xxxx inv. č. 557

str. —   , č.   61   , roku   1867

Meno   Michal Schirilla
Dátum narodenia   12. október 1867
Dátum krstu   13. október 1867
Miesto narodenia a č. domu   Poráč, č. domu neuvedené
Pohlavie   mužské
Legitimnosť   manželský

Meno rodičov, ich povolanie, náboženstvo, rodisko

Otec   Juraj Schirilla, gr. kat., roľník

Matka   Mária Cvengrosová, gr. kat.

Krstní rodičia, ich povolanie a náboženstvo   Michal Olyschavszky a Anna Olyschavszka

Svedkovia   —

Krstil   Jozef Dudinszky, miestny farár

Poznámky   —

Tento výpis sa zhoduje so zápisom v horeuvedenej matrike, ktorá je uložená v tunajšom archíve.

Riaditeľ

Vybavuje
Kredatusová
Telefón

2486 a 2424

10

**1. Coal Miners' Memorial of the Washington Mines & Coke Works
September 7 1907. Star Junction, PA** see "The Old Miner," by Raymond A. Washlaski.
(www.patheoldminer.rootsweb.ancestry.com)

(Some names from the "S" list:)
Sheney, John
(Slav. Miner, 1899. Washington Coal & Coke Company Mine, at Star Junction, Fayette Co., PA); Injured in the Washington Coal and Coke Co Mine at Star Junction, May 15, 1899. Eye struck by a piece of coal and had to be removed. (from *"The Connellsville Courier,"* Connellsville, PA May 19, 1899.)

Simon, James
(Hungarian Miner, Mule Driver ca. 1907, Washington No. 2 Mine, Fayette Co., PA Age 47. Single.); Killed by being crushed between a mine car and a room pillar in the Washington No. 2 Mine, Sept. 7, 1907.

Sirilla, Mike
(Miner, Washington Mines, Fayette Co., PA.)

Skiles, Archibald Bishop
(Miner, ca. 1900. Washington Mines, Fayette Co., PA); Thumb taken off by a fall of slate at the face of a pillar, Washington No. 3 Mine, Oct. 24, 1907.

Somerville, Robert
(Scotch Miner, Pick Miner ca. 1902. Washington Mine. Fayette Co., PA Age 50, Married.); Instantly killed by a fall of slate in the Washington Mine No. 2, Nov. 27, 1902.)

2. Deaths from the *Uniontown Herald* newspaper

(Some names from the "S" list:)
Sirgey Ellie: 81594: Morrisdale Mines: Sept. 19.

Sirgpfritz, Samuel B.: 29862; Schuylkill Co.: March 13.

Sirila, Mike: 108022: North Union: Nov. 2 (Author's note: Mike died on 02 Nov 1908 of black lung.)

Excerpted Lyrics from the song by Kathy Mattea called
"Black Lung" from the CD Called *Coal*, 2008.

**He's had more hard luck than most men could stand.
The mines was his first love, but never his friend.
He's lived a hard life and hard he'll die.
Black lung's done got him, his time is nigh.**

November, 1908

"We must look to the future with hope and not to the past with bitterness."

Left to right:
Back row: Michael, Justina, Katherine, Maria, Helen, Sophie.
Front row: Anna, Mother Maria holding Susanna, Joseph.   Author's archive.

Author's note: At the time of death of Michael Sirilla, both daughters, Katharine and Maria, back row, were already married. Daughters Anna and Helen did not accompany Mária and the remaining five children, Michael, Justina, Joseph, Sophie, Susanna, back to the ancestral village of Poráč in 1909.

November 10, 1908 Lemont Furnace, PA   *Hospodin je môj pastier, nebudem mat' nedostatku.*
                                           (The Lord is my shepherd; I shall not want.)

Moja drahá Matka, (My dear Mother) Poráč #46, Slovensko

Praise be to Jesus Christ and greetings from your daughter Mária Širila. I write of very, very sad news from Pennsylvania. My husband Michal died eight days ago, November 2, 1908, of "Black Lung," the feared coal miner's bronchial pneumonia.

He was brought home from the Washington mine around noon on November 1ˢᵗ by two of his fellow miners because he had collapsed at the bottom of the mine.   Fortunately he was working with a friend blasting when the collapse happened.   His friends carried him up the trail from the mine to our house and laid him on the bed in the living room. The company doctor came soon, but he told me that the black lung had progressed so far that there was no hope for survival. You cannot imagine my shock to know that my Michal was going to die. I took the two young children, Justína and Susana, to the neighbor's and stayed by Michal until the older children returned from school. Of course they were in shock to see their father lying on the bed in the living room, barely able to breathe, in and out of sleep. I had each one go to him individually and say a prayer and hold his hand, and he nodded to each one, knowing that he could barely speak by now.

It was later that night, as I was still at his side, praying that he wouldn't leave me, that I completely lost control of myself and screamed, " *Ježiš, Mária. Michal prosím, neopúšťáj ma. Ako budem vychorávat' tieto deti bez otca.*" (**Jesus, Mary. Michal don't leave me! How will I raise these children without a father?**) He smiled and looked at me with those clear blue Slovak eyes and said, *"Mária, vy ste moja žena a l'ubím vás. Boh sa o vás postará."* (Mária, you are my wife and I love you. God will take care of you.) He closed his eyes for the last time. It was 12 o'clock midnight.

I took his prayer book out of his hands as the tears flowed out of my eyes on to the prayer printed in the open book: *Otče náš, ktorý si na nebesiach. (*Our Father who art in heaven.) I then recited the whole prayer. I asked God to give me strength when the children awake, when I will have to tell them their father has died. I can't help but wonder what God had in mind to send such a devil, this black lung, to take my Michal away from me and the children.   Michal spent his short life digging coal for the boss. It is even sadder that he died on *Dušičky* (All Soul's Day), November 2ⁿᵈ.

The neighbor women prepared the body for visitation that occurred here in our living room. I was so thankful for their help since my mind was a blur. A 24 hour watch was made over Michal's body and a candle burned continuously next to his body. Bread and water were placed on the table next to him for nourishment for the spirit. Dear Mother, I know you know these traditions.   After three days of visitation, Michal's coffin was taken by horse carriage to St. Stephen's Greek Catholic Church in Leisenring for a funeral mass and burial in the church cemetery.   *Nech odpočíva v pokoji.* (May he rest in peace.) The day after the burial the foreman from Michal's company, H.C.Frick Coke Company, knocked on my door and handed me a letter:

> **Dear Mrs. Širila: this residence is no longer available for you and your children.**
> **Your husband, Michal Širila, our former employee, is dead.**

Dear Mother, my children and I are without a roof. I must come back and stay with you in Poráč, or stay with sister Katka in Koterbachy. It's a very long journey from Pennsylvania to Slovakia, but I know the way. I will bring 5 of my 7 dependent children with me and leave about the first of February.   My dear Mother, I am sending you greetings and wishes for a holy Christmas and a healthy New Year.

Your loving daughter, Mária   (I am sending you a photo of my family taken after Michal's burial.)

Michael Sirila: Death Certificate (Fayette County, PA)
& Grave Site (Leisenring, PA)

Form V. S. No. 5.—50M-1-16-08.

PLACE OF DEATH.

County of Fayette

Township of No. Union

or

Borough of

or

City of

[If death occurs away from USUAL RESIDENCE give facts called for under "Special Information."]

FULL NAME Mike Sirila

Registration District No. 576

Primary Registration District No. 2667

COMMONWEALTH OF PENNSYLVANIA.
BUREAU OF VITAL STATISTICS.
CERTIFICATE OF DEATH.

108022

File No.

Registered No. 780

(No. __ St.; __ Ward)

[If death occurred in a Hospital or Institution, give its NAME instead of street and number.]

PERSONAL AND STATISTICAL PARTICULARS

SEX Male | COLOR White

DATE OF BIRTH
(Month) (Day) (Year) 1

AGE 42 years, __ months, __ days.

SINGLE, MARRIED, WIDOWED, OR DIVORCED Married

BIRTHPLACE (State or County) Russia

OCCUPATION Laborer

NAME OF FATHER Unknown

BIRTHPLACE OF FATHER (State or County) " "

MAIDEN NAME OF MOTHER " "

BIRTHPLACE OF MOTHER (State or County) " "

THE ABOVE STATED PERSONAL PARTICULARS ARE TRUE TO THE BEST OF MY KNOWLEDGE AND BELIEF

(Informant) Mary Sirila

(Address) Lemont, Pa

Filed Nov 3 190 8

Registrar

MEDICAL CERTIFICATE OF DEATH

DATE OF DEATH Nov. 2 1908
(Month) (Day) (Year)

I HEREBY CERTIFY, That I attended deceased from on Nov 1st 1908 to Nov 2 1908

that I last saw him alive on Nov 1st 1908

and that death occurred, on the date stated above, at 12:00

__ M. The CAUSE OF DEATH was as follows:

A.M.

Bronchial Pneumonia (Duration) 7 Days

Contributory

(Duration) __ Days

(Signed) John D. Sturgeon M. D.

Nov 3 1908 (Address) Dunbar Pa

SPECIAL INFORMATION only for Hospitals, Institutions, Transients, or Recent Residents.

Former or Usual Residence __ How long at Place of Death __ ?Days

Where was disease contracted?

PLACE OF BURIAL OR REMOVAL | DATE OF BURIAL
Leisenring #1 | Nov 4 190 8

UNDERTAKER | ADDRESS
Jos. Haky | Uniontown Pa

Author's photo
Author's note: Mike's birthplace on his death certificate
was incorrectly written as Russia. It should have been
Poráč which was Hungary at the time.

PART ONE – PORÁČ

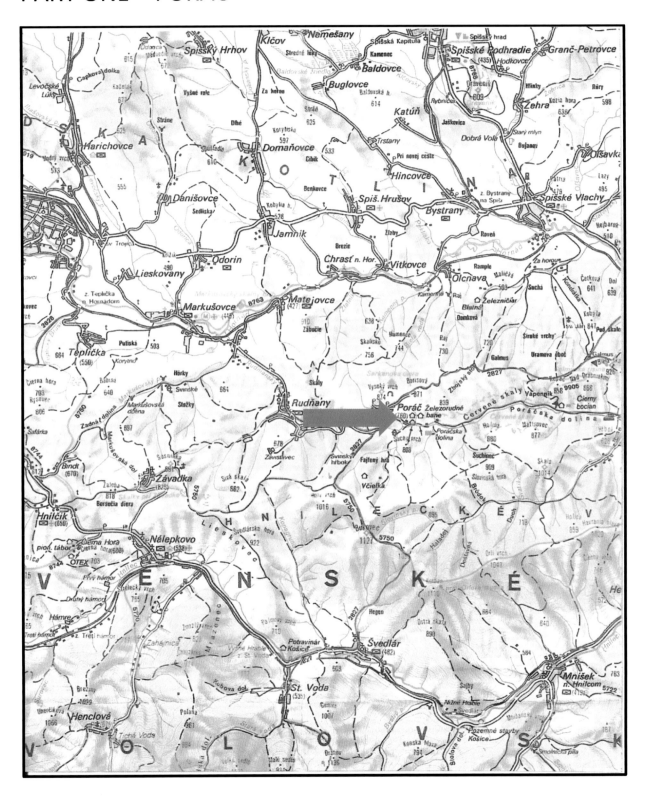

Mária Mrozko & Family

Photo Abt 1908 at #46, Poráč.
Left to right:
Mária Jureková (1898-1933) daughter of Martin & Katarína Ďurica Jurek;
Mária Mrozko Ďurica (1849-1913) grandmother;
Helena Ďuricková (1893-1985), youngest child of Mária Ďurica;
Katarína Ďurica Jurek (1876-1947), third daughter of Mária Ďurica;
Baby Michal Jurek (1907-1910, son of Martin & Katarína Jurek
Š. Cvengroš archive.

Stephanus Schirilla

*Photo of Stephanus Schirilla (05 Mar 1858 – 17 May 1932),
brother to Michal Sirilla's father, Juraj Schirilla (1834-1932),
near his residence at #41, Poráč. His spouse was Mária Barbuš.
Courtesy of the Tucci Family Tree, www.ancestry.com*

*Author's note: This photo is included because there has been no
photo of Mária's husband, Michael Sirilla, or any other Sirilla
relatives located so far.*

Train route from Bremen, Germany to Poráč

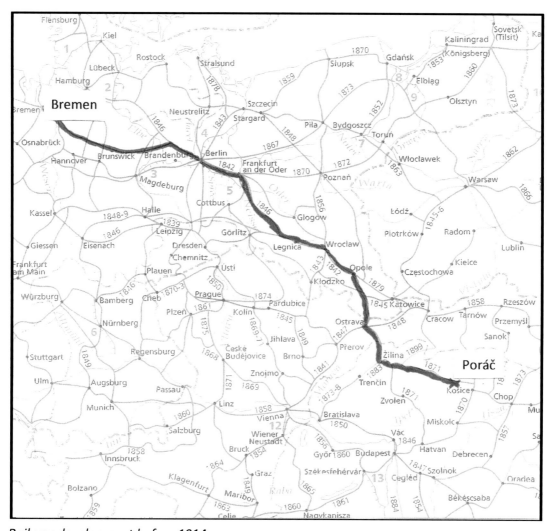

Railway development before 1914.
Courtesy of Historical Atlas of East Central Europe by Paul Robert Magocsi, p. 91.
Permission from the author.

Poráč in February. Author's archive.

February 15, 1909, Poráč, *still called Vereshegy, (pronounced in Hungarian Vereshhedge)*
Aká si mi krásna, ty rodná zem moja.
(How beautiful you are, O land of my birth.)

My dearest sister Anna, at home in Brownfield, PA

I am writing from our home #46 in Poráč. I know you are wondering about our journey and how I managed to keep control of 5 children on this very long trip from Pennsylvania. I and my 5 children arrived safely, although it was a very long, long journey. The ship's time was 10 days, and Sophie was a big help, especially with the two boys who loved to run all over the upper deck. I spent most of my time in our quarters in steerage with Baby Zuzana, and 3-year-old Justína. My ticket for the voyage was about $30 and it allowed 4 children to travel free. In Bremenhaven we were able to take a horse drawn taxi to Bremen, stay overnight in a dormitory and from there the next morning get a non-stop train to Berlin. The children slept most of the way, and from Berlin we were able to get a night train from Berlin to Bohumín where we changed for the train going to Košice. However, we were able to depart at Markušovce where Martin, sister Katka's husband, met us with his wagon and drove us to Koterbachy (later called Rudňany) where we all were reunited with family once more. We slept and slept for two days and then made the short journey to Poráč in Martin's wagon to our mother's house.

Mama complains of pains in her chest, but she is most gracious in accepting 5 children and a daughter in her home. What else could I do after the eviction from our home after Michal's death? You would not believe how empty is Poráč now because so many of our family and other families have emigrated. It is like a ghost town. The Hungarians insist on the use of their language (Magyar) outside of home, in schools, and government offices. Sophie, Michael, and Joseph are attending the village school, and their classes are taught only in Hungarian. My poor children know only Slovak and English! We speak Slovak at home but never on the street. Even the priest in our St. Demeter's Greek Catholic Church must use Hungarian language in his sermons. He can still use Old Slavonic in the mass, thank goodness.

How are my growing girls, Anna and Helen? Again, I thank you for keeping them while we are gone. I hope they are not homesick for the rest of us here in Slovakia. You know the living standards here are not that much different from living in the Patch in Fayette County. There we had no inside running water, we had to use a privy outside, bathing was minimal, washing clothes was very hard, and we had to grow as many vegetables and fruit as possible during the summer to have something to eat during the winter. Also, we had our own chickens and geese to provide eggs and feathers for pillows and comforters. Here it is the same! The big difference is that here H.C. Frick & Coke Co does not own the house and garden! Here too Mama has a cow for milk and one pig a year for slaughter for ham and bacon.

I love to walk with Baby Zuza and my Justína to the end of our narrow street and gaze east at Spišský hrad, the largest castle in central Europe, and then if I am out at sunset to gaze west at the setting sun behind the Tatra Mountains. Also at the very end of the village are the sheep stalls where the wonderful *bryndza* (sheep's cheese) is made. There is no meal in all of Pennsylvania that tastes as good as Slovak sheep's cheese with potato dumplings: **bryndzové halušky.** Mama fixes this for all of us at least twice a week and the children devour it.

I was hoping to meet a widower here in Poráč who would welcome a new widow as wife, but you already know how Poráč is practically empty of men! Be sure to mention to Father Dzubay at St. Stephen's Church in Leisenring that I am a widow needing to remarry. Any help that the Greek Catholic Union could give would also be appreciated. I am grateful for their assistance with our travel costs.

I know Poráč is a very great distance from Pennsylvania, but in our hearts you are always very close. I hope you will write and tell us news of the rest of our family. I don't miss anything about coal mining. My Michal's death and the deaths of husbands of other wives have soured me. Here in Poráč, I am enjoying the wonderful pure air and don't miss the haze, smut, and dirt from the coal mines, especially the heat blasting from the coke ovens running 24 hours a day.   Nor do I miss the sound of the disaster bell that all of us dreaded so much that told us of accidents or too often death.

I'm still grieving the loss of my husband. I feel my heart is a stone, but I have no tears. I am fine while asleep, but when I wake up I have a vision of the foreman delivering the eviction letter, and then I see a vision of Michal's casket being lowered into the ground. That's when I cry out, "Why, Oh Lord, Why?" I don't miss anything about coal mining. We all send you Hugs and Kisses from Porác.

Your loving sister, Mária and children: Sophie, Michael, Joseph, Justína, and Baby Zuzana!!!!
And our Mama and sister Helena (and Žižka, the cat) give you their one hundred kisses!!

Hutzul Kitchen, by Ukrainian American artist Yaroslava Surmach Mills. (1925-2008)
Painting on Glass, 1980. Courtesy from reprinted notecard by Surma Book & Music Co
New York. Permission granted from the Yaraslava Mills estate, 2018.

This could be the Ďurica house #46 in Poráč.
Members of the Širilla and Ďurica families are as follows:
Left to right: Jozef, Mária (Mother), Žofia, Justína, Zuzana
Top to Bottom: Michal, Mária (Grandmother), Helena (Sister), Žížka (cat)

May lst, 1909, #46, Poráč, Slovakia   *Nech sa páči.* (Go ahead. Help yourself.)

My dearest sister Anna,
Many thanks for your lovely Easter greeting from Brownfield. Here we celebrated Easter according to the Julian calendar on March 29. I know your Easter was on the Gregorian calendar on April 11. We dyed eggs (*pysanky*) and decorated our food basket for the priest to bless.

I am happy to hear that my girls, Anna and Helen, are adjusting to our absence. Please tell them that we hope to return to Pennsylvania at the end of the summer, which pleases the children very much. I have received a letter confirming that I can work as a domestic with a family in Uniontown, although there will not be housing offered at the family's residence. I have suggested that our sister Helena, who is now almost 16, accompany us back to Pennsylvania. She seems willing but with the idea that she would return to Poráč since Mama is not healthy. My two younger girls will still need care at home (the older five children will be in school), so sister Helena would be a big help when we return.

One evening we were all sitting by the big ceramic stove, stripping goose feathers for another feather quilt (*perina),* (well, the boys were mostly giggling and causing feathers to fly all over the room) when Michael, our studious one, asked me what was life like for Babka (Mária Mrozko) and Dedo (Michal Ďurica) here in Poráč. I thought, yes, this story is important for the children to remember. Oh, Anna, so many memories. I began with the story of our parents' marriage on
November 14, 1870
And then my birth, their first child, born on
November 20, 1871
After me came Anna, then Katarína, then Elíáš, then Matej, then Ján, then Michal, then Helena. A total of 8 children, all living at #46, this same house in Poráč. It is customary for the bride to live with the groom's family after marriage, so this was the Ďurica home where our mother's "in-laws" lived, along with 5 hectares of land for crops like oats, wheat, barley, potatoes, flax, and sugar beets. In 1890, my parents felt that I should marry, and since a Michal Širila, from #10A, had just returned from working as a coal miner in Hubbard, Ohio, he was eligible. We married on
July 21, 1890
This was an arranged marriage, and we began our life together with the Širila family. It was soon after that that Michal's brother, Štefan, decided to go back to Hubbard, Ohio where an uncle, Ján Cvengroš (a brother of their mother, Mária Cvengroš) was working in a blast furnace, and according to his letters, he was making lots of money. Before we married, Michal told me that he *might* want to return to Ohio because there were jobs there, unlike here in Poráč where men sit out on the stoop all day because in 1880 the mines here were shut down. By the new year, 1891, I was expecting our first child. Michal wanted to return to Hubbard, Ohio, so we decided that the best thing was for me to stay in Poráč, have the baby, then Michal would send me money for the ship's journey to Hubbard. So in the early part of 1891 Michal left, but without official papers called "permission to emigrate." In Bremenhaven, it took him 3 tries to get on a ship. Finally the last try was successful because he dressed as a woman and gave a false name. Meanwhile I gave birth to Baby Mária in Poráč on
May 22, 1891
As the months passed, I never received any letter or money from Michal, so I wrote to his uncle who then sent me money for the ship's passage. My sister Anna accompanied me because she was already engaged to marry Josef Sopkovič, from Rudňany, who had already emigrated to Pennsylvania. My Michal was living in a boarding house with all Slovak men who liked to drink vodka and slivovica after work. So Michal was not happy to see me and Baby Mária. By March of 1892, I was expecting our

second baby, and it was then that Michal **demanded** that I return to Poráč and **wait** until he either sent for me or came himself to Poráč. Baby Katarína was born in Poráč on

September 8, 1892

So I stayed at #46, the Ďurica house, for 4 years and only seldom heard from Michal. Finally in 1896 he arrived in Poráč, a complete surprise! Because of our 4 year separation, we were like strangers, but we decided to go back to Ohio together with the two baby girls because he still had his job at the coal mine and was entitled to company housing since we were a family. He encouraged his brother Ján to emigrate and sail with us. So we all left Poráč, and Ján, I, and the two girls sailed from Bremenhaven on the ship *Spree*, arriving in New York at Ellis Island on

February 6, 1896

Michal was unable to get passage on the *Spree*, so he waited and got passage on the ship *Bonn*, arriving in New York at Ellis Island on **February 18, 1896**

From New York we all traveled directly to Hubbard, Ohio where Michal resumed his coal mining job, and we received company housing. It was during this time that Sophie was born, on **March 7, 1897,** and the day after her birth, the mine in Hubbard closed, so we all left for Lemont, Pennsylvania where Michal was able to get a job as a coal miner for the H.C. Frick Coal and Coke Company. We moved into company miners' housing in Lemont Furnace, and it was there in Lemont that the rest of you were born:

Michael (Oct. 6, 1898); Joseph (March 2, 1900); Anna (Jan. 1, 1902); Helen (July 16, 1903); Justina (March 16, 1905); Nicholas (Nov. 15, 1906 who died as an infant); and Susanna (Dec. 14, 1907).

We housed anywhere from 4-6 men as boarders in our company housing, mostly Slovaks we knew from Poráč, and I cooked for them, washed their clothes for them, and cleaned their room because we absolutely needed the money they paid us. The best part of this period was the religious holidays and gatherings with other Slovaks who belonged to St. Stephen's Church in Leisenring.

We all know how this part of the story ends: with the death of your father from Black Lung on **November 2, 1908** in Lemont, Pennsylvania, and now we start a new chapter.

Anna, I'm enclosing these Slovak stamps. Each one resembles one of my children.
Your loving sister, Mária

Žofia	**Michal**	**Jozef**	**Justina**	**Zuzana**
helpful	curious	mischievous	loving	playful
nápomocný	*dôkladý*	*nezbedný*	*ľúbiaci*	*hravý*

Papercuts by the Czech artist, Kornelie Némecková, Prague, Czech Republic.

Within Poráč

Author's photos.

Remembrances of Poráč

Sophie's *poličkovanie čipka*
(bobbin lace)

Michael's *fujara*
(shepherd's flute)

Justina's *Morena bábika*
(morena doll)

Joseph's *Fašiangy maska*
(carnival mask)

Susanna's *Veľká noc keks*
(Easter cookies)

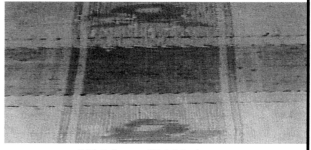

Helena's *perina*
(feather quilt)

Mária's poráčský koberec
(Poráč rag rug)

Author's archive.

August 1, 1909, Poráč #46   *Slniečko sa rado díva do domu.*   (The sun loves to see into the home.)

My dearest sister Anna,
We are hoping to leave Poráč at the end of August, and the sailing time is now 10 days. The children should be able to resume their school classes in Pennsylvania without too much delay, although Sophie doesn't want to attend school anymore, and the boys say they are ready to work in the mines.   I have sold my "dowry acreage" so that I can pay for the ship's passage and the transportation from New York to Uniontown. Also our sister Helena will leave with us as will several other families from Poráč.

I have told the children that they can choose one item to bring back to the US from Poráč that tells their favorite memory of our stay here. So here is what they chose:

Sophie wants to bring back her new friend, Andrej Liška, our neighbor, who is 14 and thinks that working in a coal mine in Pennsylvania for 20 cents an hour is better than staying at home doing nothing here in Poráč! Well, we can't take him along, so Sophie chose a bobbin lace lady that one of the Ďurica relatives made and gave her as a present for her birthday on March 7th.

Michael has spent many hours helping out at the sheep barn and has seen the shepherds playing the *fujara,* (the traditional Slovak bassoon) so he wants to bring one back to Pennsylvania. It is quite long, and I don't know if it can be cut into pieces so that he can pack it, but we will see. I think it will be quite a showpiece in Fayette County.

Joseph, our mischievous one, wants to bring back a mask that he wore during the Fašiangy Carnival Parade.   Remember our childhood *Fašiangy* just before Lent when we dressed up in strange outfits and marched in a parade throughout the village. The parade is still a popular event here in Poráč just like when we were children.   So Joseph's mask could be a showpiece too in Fayette County.

Justina wants to bring her doll which now has a new name, *Morena*, because she saw the girls in town on May 1st walking with the stuffed Morena lady on a stick and singing their special song about throwing the Morena into the river, meaning that winter is over. So she renamed her doll Morena.

Susanna is still much the baby, so she would like to bring along some lovely decorated cookies that Babka baked for her for Easter.

Our sister **Helena** wants to bring her *perina*, (feather quilt). It's bulky, but it would be perfect for the 10 days on the ship and very warm once we settle in for the winter in Fayette County!

And I hope I can fit a small handwoven Poráč rag rug in my pack, as a remembrance of our stay with Mama.   I made it myself on Mama's loom and hope someday that I will have a loom myself to create these precious rag rugs, where each Slovak village has its own special pattern.

Anna, we have much work to do in helping with the harvest before we pack for our very long journey. Katka's husband Martin Jurek will come with his wagon from Koterbachy (Rudňany) and will drive us to Markušovce where we will board the train for Bohumín. Then we will transfer to a train headed for Berlin and then on to Bremen where we can have bunkhouse sleeping accommodations until our ship is ready to sail. We hope to see you in September. Pray for us. *Všetko najlepšie.* (Everything is O.K.)

Your loving sister, Mária

Return to New York

Required by the regulations of the Secretary of Commerce and Labor of the United States, under Act of Congress approved February 20, 1907, to be delivered

S.S. *Bremen* sailing from *Bremen* August 21 1909

Courtesy of Ellis Island Passengers' List

S.S. BREMEN, 1897 North German Lloyd
Courtesy The Peabody Museum of Salem

August 28, 1909 Bremerhaven, Germany   *Slovensko moje, otčina moja* (My Slovakia, my fatherland)

My dearest sister Anna,

We arrived safely in Bremerhaven, but it was a very, very long journey from Poráč, especially for the children. We are just leaving port now, sailing on the ship *Bremen* and are scheduled to arrive in New York on September 7th, if weather permits. We watched two little tugs pulling the huge ship away from the dock, while above the screaming sea gulls yelled madly as the ship moved up the Weser River towards the sea. I gazed at the shore of Europe with a heavy heart, knowing that I may never return to my beloved Poráč. I stared and stared as long as land was in sight thinking about our village and the hardships caused by the Hungarian submission there now, and I watched my Europe fade into memory. As you know, this is my third time leaving Europe: first in 1891, then in 1896 and now in 1909. Sometimes I wonder, "Where is my home?"

My mind relived our goodbyes. First, all of the children hugged and kissed their *Babka* (Grandma) goodbye. Then it was our sister Helena's turn. She hugged Mama and told her not to cry because she will for sure return to Poráč. As Helena glanced at me, both she and I doubted she would return; the village was almost empty of young marriageable men who had left for jobs in the coal mines of Pennsylvania. It was like a broom came along and swept away half of the residents of our village, especially the young men. Helena probably would not return. Then I walked to Mama, trying to sound brave and said, *"Moja drahá matka, spomeň si na mňa vždy."* (My dear mother, remember me always.) She slowly came to me and made the sign of the cross on my forehead and said, with tears falling from her eyes, *"Dovidenia moja dcéra. Nech Pán Boch žehná moje dieta, v mene Otca, Syna, a Svätého Ducha."* (Goodbye my daughter. May God bless you, my child, in the name of the Father, the Son, and the Holy Ghost.) I threw my arms around her and thanked her for her help during these past months. My own tears fell on the soil that I probably would never see again. Our sister Katka took me to her husband Martin's wagon where the children, sister Helena, and almost the entire village were waiting, or what was left of Poráč after these years of emigration. Everyone was waving and wishing us a safe voyage, as the sun rose over Spišský hrad (Spiš Castle) in the east. The roosters were crowing the beginning of a new day, the cows were mooing, needing to be milked, and the sheep at the bryndza barn were baaing their need for attention, too. I think every person and animal belonging to Poráč was awake to say their goodbyes.

In Markušovce, Martin helped us board a train coming from Košice for Bohumín. He stopped in front of the Renaissance manor built in 1643, connected with the Hungarian Máriássy family. In Europe there is always history!

Anna, I got a glimpse of the manifest as we were boarding the ship. I will try to tell you what I saw and how all the notations were all in Hungarian. Our beloved **Poráč** was listed by the Hungarian name, **Vereshegy.** All of our names were written in Hungarian: I was listed as **Mihalyne Sirilla,** (which translates into the wife of Mihaly, Michal). (Helena's family name was listed as Sirilla, when it should have been Ďurica.) The children's names were all spelled in Hungarian: **Zsofia** (Sophie); **Mihaly** (Michael); **Jozsef** (Joseph); **Justina** (Justina); and **Zsuzsanna** (Suzanna). Don't tell anyone but there are whispers in Poráč of a possible uprising against the Hungarians. Imagine!

Our destination is Uniontown, and we will stay with daughter Katie and husband John Duritsa in Lemont. I will mail this letter to you from New York.

Zbohom. (God be with you.) Your loving sister, Mária

"Mother of Exiles"

Give me your tired, your poor,
Your huddled masses yearning to breathe free,
The wretched refuse of your teeming shore.
Send these, the homeless, tempest-tost to me,
I lift my lamp beside the golden door!

*By Emma Lazarus, inscribed on the base of
The Statue of Liberty.*

Author's photo.

The U.S. Mint's Quarters' National
Parks Series for 2017 is of Ellis Island
National Park.

1909.
Back Row: Helena Ďurica, Sophie and Michael Sırılla
Front Row: Sirillas: Joseph, Mária, Susanna, and Justina.
Author's archive.

28

September 7, 1909 New York, USA   *Čas je drahý.* (Time is precious.)

My dearest sister Katka, at #261 Koterbachy, (Rudňany), Slovakia
We were 10 days at sea sharing the most simple accommodations in steerage with other travelers from all over central and eastern Europe: Jews persecuted by Russians; Poles and Serbs persecuted by Austrians; Croats and Slovaks persecuted by Hungarians; and even Irish persecuted by English. There is no common language between us, but there is a common thought: <u>hope</u> for a better life in Ameryka. Our ticket says our ship *Bremen* can hold 1,850 persons in steerage. I truly believe that we are more than that. In lst and 2nd class it says the ship can hold at each level about 250. Because the boys have been all over the ship exploring all of the decks, they have been able to speak English with many of the passengers of the lst and 2nd decks and according to some of these passengers, someone as famous as the American writer Mark Twain was a lst class passenger in 1907, two years ago, on this very ship, the *Bremen*! The boys seem to know who this Mark Twain is!!

We had a small room with 3 bunks on each side and a toilet far down the hallway that served most of the passengers in steerage and opened into the sea. Our bunks were not very high and did not allow the sleeper to sit up in bed. So here was our arrangement for the first night: Bunk # l: top, Helena, middle, Justina; bottom, me and Baby Zuza. Bunk #2: top, Sophie, middle, Michael, bottom, Joseph. This didn't work because Helena on the top of bunk #1 was vomiting all night as was Sophie on the top of bunk #2. So we had to rearrange everyone: Bunk #1: top, Joseph, middle, me and Baby Zuza , bottom, Helena. Bunk #2: top, Michael, middle, Justina, bottom, Sophie. Our second arrangement worked better, putting the boys on the top bunks so no one had to put sawdust over fresh vomit that missed the can. The German maid, Eva, was also good about cleaning up every morning. Our meals were served in an area just for steerage passengers, and they were not very tasty.

Since it is easy at sea to lose track of time, and we were told our voyage was to be 10 days, we found a long piece of string and tied it to the top bunk. At the end of each day before going to sleep, we placed a knot in the string so that we could keep track of the days. When any child said, "Mama, how many more days until we get to New York?" I said, "Just count the knots and subtract from 10!" We had only one bad storm day, thank God.

At the end of day 10, we heard everyone running up on the 2nd class deck because we were in sight of New York City, and everyone wanted to see at last the "Beautiful Lady," the Statue of Liberty. The sounds of awe as we heard "There she is!" in so many different languages put tears to my eyes. For almost everyone in steerage, except us, this was the first time to see in person this Statue. We could also hear many people trying to pronounce the words in English at the base of the Statue. What made our group different from the other steerage passengers was that we were not entering this harbor for the first time. For me this was the **third** time, and for the children, they had all left New York through this harbor in February eight months ago.   Also, the children speak English to each other, and that also made us unique since NO other children in steerage spoke English. I hope my older children will always remember this voyage.

The exit strategy for the *Bremen* was for lst and 2nd class passengers to get health and security clearance on board, so that when we docked, they were able to press the door that said "This way to New York City" almost immediately. We steerage passengers went by ferry to Ellis Island for health and security clearance and sometimes this meant waiting several hours in steerage before being called to board the ferry. Also each passenger had a number on his/her coat that corresponded to the individual's ticket number.

At Ellis Island the health exams were intense, the worst being the test for trachoma, a contagious eye disease. An assistant would raise and turn the eyelid up to check inside the eye for inflammation. Some assistants would use an instrument for turning up the eyelid!! This hurt, and many children including ours could not stop crying. There were other health concerns: lice, lameness, scalp diseases, skin diseases, and mental incapacity. If the passenger was diagnosed with one of these, a mark was placed on the back of his/ her coat, and this meant reexamination. Also all of the questions from the manifest asked in Bremerhaven were asked again here at Ellis Island. So the process was very long and tiring, especially for the children. Fortunately, all of us passed all of the tests, and we were then escorted to a waiting area where women without male accompaniment had to wait for a male relative for pick up. This was for the woman's own security.

While we were waiting, I slipped my hand again into my left pocket and touched the picture and prayer of the Blessed Virgin which Mama had put in my pocket for good luck. I know this long journey is over, but the memory of our stay in Poráč will never be lost.

We were so happy to see my daughter's husband, John Duritsa, who claimed us and escorted us by train to Pittsburgh, then on to Uniontown, and last to our former patch house in the coal town of Lemont. We will stay there getting to know my two daughters again, Anna and Helen, who did not travel with us to Poráč, as you know. When the mining company required me and my children to leave this house after Michael's death, this house was taken by my daughter Katie and her husband, John Duritsa. John works at the Washington mine, so he was entitled to company housing. Katie and John said they will not take in any boarders because accommodating me and 7 children will fill the house! For this I am very grateful .

 Katka, I know you know all of my secrets, and my one secret wish for being in Poráč was to find a widower there to marry. In our custom it is still common that if the deceased husband had a single brother, it was that brother's obligation to marry the widow. Well, the only brother of Michael's left in Poráč is Juráj, as you know, and he is happily married with a family to raise. All the other brothers have emigrated and are married. So, I am not asking for pity, just thinking that my best possibility of finding a widower will be to ask the priest at St. Stephen's Church here in Leisenring to look out for me. Katka, pray for me, please.

Despite all of my gloomy talk, I will be very happy to be back in Fayette County, but I know that as a widow with these 7 dependent children this will be a difficult time. And of course now I will miss you and your family in Rudňany and our Mama now alone in Poráč. The very hardest thing about returning to Pennsylvania is the memory of leaving my family across this enormous ocean. I am truly torn "between two cultures."

Zbohom. (God be with you.)
Your loving sister,
Mária

The Connellsville
Coke Region

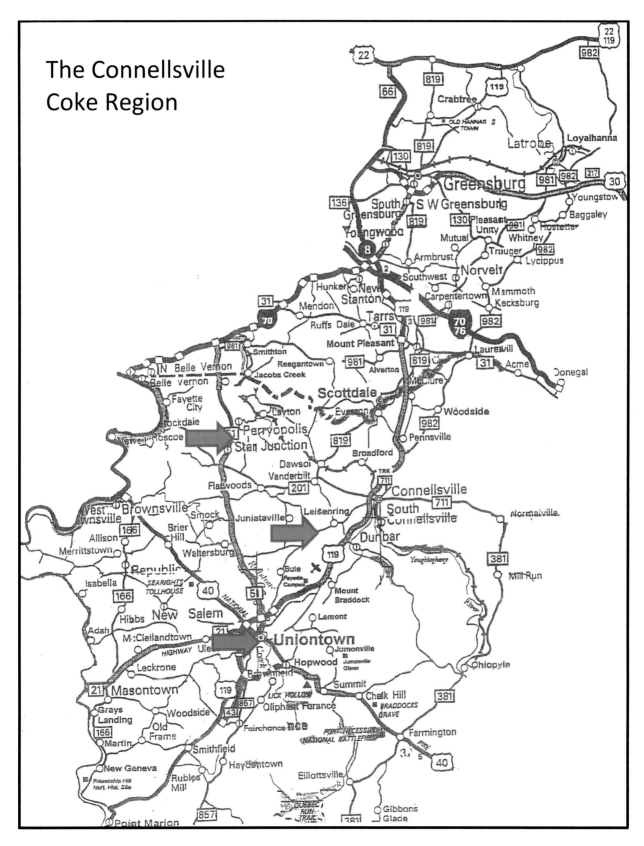

It's not that you are in the story, it's the story in you.

Patch Duplex, Lemont Furnace, PA   Abt 1920.   Author's archive.

Patch Duplex, Lemont Furnace , PA Abt 1910. Author's photo.

75th Anniversary Booklet (1892-1967)
St. Stephen's Byzantine Catholic Church
Leisenring, PA

Mária Dursa

First Ladies' Lodge: Abt 1910.

Michael Sirilla

Justina Sirilla

First School Class: Abt 1910.

No. 22930

APPLICATION FOR MARRIAGE LICENSE.

1. Full name of the man,	*Mike Dursa*	14. Previously married, how often—woman,	*Once*
2. Full name of the woman,	*Mary Serilla*	15. Date of death of man's former wife, if any,	*Feby. 1907*
3. Relationship of the parties, either by blood or marriage,	*None*	16. Date of death of woman's former husband, if any,	*Nov. 1908*
4. Age of the man,	*34*	17. Date of divorce of man at any time,	*None*
5. Age of the woman,	*38*	18. Cause of divorce of man,	*None*
6. Residence of the man,	*Star Junction Pa.*	19. Date of divorce of woman at any time,	*None*
7. Residence of the woman,	*Lemont "*	20. Cause of divorce of woman,	*None*
8. Parents' names—man,	*John and Annie*	21. Color of parties,	*White*
9. Parents' names—woman,	*Mike " Mary.*	22. Occupation of man,	*Miner* MINE
10. Guardian's name—man,	*None*	23. Occupation of woman,	*Domestic*
11. Guardian's name—woman,	*None*	24. Place of birth—man,	*Austria*
12. Consent of parents or guardian,	*None*	25. Place of birth—woman,	*Austria.*
13. Previously married, how often—man,	*Once*		

FAYETTE COUNTY, SS:

Personally appeared before me *Clk of O.C.* *Mike Dursa* of said County of Fayette, at Pa, *Mary Serilla* and who, being duly qualified according to law, did depose and say that the statements above set forth are correct and true, to the best of their knowledge and belief.

Sworn and subscribed before me this

18 day of *July* A.D. 19*10*

Chas. O. Schroyer
Clerk Orphans' Court.

Mike x Dursa
her
meri x Serilla

No. 22930

MARRIAGE LICENSE.

State of Pennsylvania, County of Fayette, ss:

To any Minister of the Gospel, Justice of the Peace, or other Officers or Persons authorized by Law to Solemnize Marriage:

You are hereby authorized to join together in the holy state of matrimony, according to the rites and ceremonies of your church, society or religious denomination and the laws of the Commonwealth of Pennsylvania *Mike Dursa* and *Mary Serilla*

Given under my hand and the the Seal of the Orphans' Court of said County of Fayette, at Uniontown, this *18* day of *July*. A.D. 19*10*

Chas. A. Schroyer
Clerk.

No. 22930

DUPLICATE CERTIFICATE.

I, *Rev N. Stecovich* hereby certify that on the *19* day of *July* one thousand nine hundred and *Ten* at *New Salem Pa.* *Mike Dursa* and *Mary Serilla* were by me united in marriage, in accordance with license issued by the Clerk of the Orphan's Court of Fayette County, Pennsylvania, numbered *22930*

When returned *Sept 27* 19*10*

Rev N. Stecovich
Minister of the Gospel, Justice of the Peace or Alderman.

No. 22930

MARRIAGE LICENSE.

State of Pennsylvania, County of Fayette, ss:

To and

Legal evidence having been furnished to me in accordance with the Act of Assembly approved the twenty-third day of June, one thousand eight hundred and eighty-five, this certifies that I am satisfied that there is no legal impediment to your joining yourselves together in marriage.

Given under my hand and the Seal of the Orphan's Court of said County of Fayette, at Uniontown, this day of A. D.

Courtesy of Fayette County Courthouse archive, Uniontown, PA

August 1, 1910, Star Junction, PA.   *V Poráči, to boli zlaté časy.* (Those were the days in Poráč.)

Moja sestra Katarína žijúca v #261 Koterbachy, Slovensko od tvojej sestry Heleny:
(To my dear sister Katarína at #261, Koterbachy, Slovakia. From your sister Helena.)

I am greeting you from Star Junction and especially asking about our Mama's health. I know the Mrozko family looks after her, but I often feel guilty for having left her alone in Poráč. Since I am the youngest of her children, I am the one child who knows her best since all the others before me (except you, Katka) left Poráč for a new life in Pennsylvania.

After our arrival in Pennsylvania in September, 1909, we lived in Lemont Furnace with my niece, Katie and her husband John Duritsa. It is the same patch house duplex that Mária and Michael Sirilla lived in before he died, when two days later the coal company evicted her and her children from the house. Katie and John were entitled to a company house since John works as a miner in the Washington mine. So John was able to lease the duplex from the coal company.

As you know, Katie was born in Poráč on September 8, 1892, and I was born in Poráč on November 19, 1893, so my niece is older than I am! Katie gave birth to her first child this May 6th, and I am learning how to care for this baby boy named George.   We call him *"Jurko"* which is Slovak for Georgie. We are all very happy to have a new baby in the family.

But the **BIG** news is that our sister Mária has remarried! Yes, on July 19, 1910, Mária and Michael Dursa were married by the Rev. Stecovich in New Salem, Pennsylvania.   Since Michael, my new brother-in –law, lives in a company house in Star Junction, we moved from Lemont to his house.   His first wife died in 1907 and they had one living child, Steve.   Michael is a "saint" to become step father to <u>seven</u> children: Sophie, Michael, Joseph, Anna, Helen, Justina, and Susanna.   And everyone loves him dearly including me. Mária becomes a step-mother to only <u>one</u>, his son, Steve.

Other big news is that I am becoming very fond of Michael Dursa's younger brother, Joseph. We first met at the wedding of a friend, and when he asked me to dance with him, I accepted and we were dancing and talking the whole evening. Later when Michael would come to visit our sister Mária, he started to bring Joseph, and that was the beginning of our courtship.

I am almost 17 years old and Joseph is 21 years old and now he wants to marry me! We think we will set the date for October 19, 1910 and will have a typical Slovak wedding held on that Saturday. It will be a *"Velka Zabava"*: a big party.

As you know, Katka, our custom back home is to ask the bride's parents for permission to marry the day before the marriage ceremony. Since I have no parents here, I will first ask permission from my sister and brother-in law to get married. Then my family, including my nieces and nephews, who will all get dressed up in their best outfits, along with Joseph's family, and the musicians, will all go by electric rail car to St. Stephen's Church in Leisenring for the sacred ceremony.   After the ceremony we will have a big Slovak dinner in the basement of the church, and the food will be prepared by the women in our family during the whole week before the ceremony.   Of course we'll have *holúbky* (stuffed cabbage), *pirohý* (cheese filled dumplings), *halušky* (potato dumplings in a sauce of sheep's cheese), potato salad, pickled beets, homemade *klobása*, (Slovak sausage), and an assortment of rolls, cookies, pies, breads and walnut and poppy seed rolled cakes. After the dinner we will have a Slovak band play for dancing. Usually the band has two accordians, a guitar, a bass fiddle and sometimes a saxophone. They will play many polkas, especially "the Pennsylvania Polka."   At the end of the evening, I will dance with anyone, as is the custom.   The person dancing with me will put money in a special hat, and this money will go to our family who paid for the wedding. I hope the men don't drink too much of their homemade *slivovica*, (plum brandy) , and *pivo* (Slovak beer), as usual, but I'm sure our *"na zdravie"* (the toast "to your health") will be given many, many times.

Katka, of course you know all of these traditions. What is missing here in our Pennsylvania is the tradition the evening before the wedding ceremony where the girlfriends of the future bride come to her house and sing the beautiful Slovak folksongs. I remember this vividly from your wedding, Katka, even though I was quite young at the time. Now my girlfriends are all in Poráč so this part of the tradition will be lost. I remember that later in the evening your future husband, Martin Jurek, and his male friends came to our house, and the girls sang the popular song, *Posledný krát t'a pobozkám, Martin* (The Last Time I Will Kiss Martin).   After that beautiful song, they threw Martin fondly into a pile of feather quilts, giggling and maybe kissing him for the last time. The house was filled with love and laughter before the serious ceremony the next day. Katka, I will send you a photo of my special day.

So now Mária has become "Mary Dursa" and I will become "Helen Dursa." What surprises does life have?   I know that life for a 21-year-old miner and his 17-year-old bride will not be easy, but we will look to the Lord for help and expect happiness here in Pennsylvania every day of our marriage.

Give my love to our Mama and to your family. I hope all of you have enjoyed a pleasant summer. Hellos from all of us here in Pennsylvania.
Your loving sister, Helena

Author's note:
On October 19, 1960 Joseph and Helen Dursa celebrated their 50th wedding anniversary, and on Sunday October 23, they renewed their nuptial vows at a high mass at St. John the Baptist Byzantine Church in Uniontown, Pennsylvania. A family dinner followed in their home at 86 Chaffee St., Uniontown, shared with their six children. Both are buried in the Hopwood Cemetery.
Joseph died November, 1975 and Helen, died December 18, 1985.

October 27, 1960. Uniontown Herald Standard.
D. Pohmurski archive.

Family Group Sheet for Helena Durica

	Husband:	Joseph Dursa
	Birth:	15 Mar 1889 in Porac, (Spis) Slovakia
	Death:	Nov 1975 in Uniontown, Fayette, PA
	Marriage:	19 Oct 1910 in Fayette County, PA
	Father:	John Dursa
	Mother:	Anna Polkabla

	Wife:	Helena Durica
	Birth:	19 Nov 1893 in Porac, (Spis) Slovakia
	Death:	19 Dec 1985 in Uniontown, Fayette, PA
	Father:	Michael Durica
	Mother:	Maria Mrozko

Children:

1 M	Name:	John Dursa
	Birth:	06 Oct 1911 in Lemont Furnace,Fayette, PA
	Death:	19 Feb 2004 in Uniontown, Fayette, PA

2 F	Name:	Mary Dursa
	Birth:	13 Aug 1913 in Lemont Furnace,Fayette, PA
	Death:	Aug 1985 in Uniontown,PA

3 F	Name:	Anna Dursa
	Birth:	09 Jul 1915 in Lemont Furnace,Fayette, PA
	Death:	20 Jan 2011 in Uniontown,Fayette, PA

4 M	Name:	Joseph Dursa Jr.
	Birth:	22 Apr 1917 in Lemont Furnace,Fayette, PA
	Death:	25 Mar 2005 in Uniontown,Fayette, PA

5 M	Name:	Michael Dursa
	Birth:	03 Nov 1919 in Lemont Furnace,Fayette, PA
	Death:	01 Sep 1928 in North Union, Fayette, PA

6 F	Name:	Margaret Dursa
	Birth:	21 Nov 1920 in Lemont Furnace,Fayette, PA
	Death:	13 Jul 2007 in Uniontown, Fayette, PA

7 M	Name:	Frank Dursa
	Birth:	02 Nov 1922 in Lemont,Fayette, PA
	Death:	03 Sep 2001 in Uniontown,Fayette, PA

Notes

DURSA

MOTHER HELEN 1893 — 1985

FATHER JOSEPH 1889 — 1975

January 10, 1911, Star Junction, PA   *To je záškret.* (It is diphtheria.)

My dearest sister Katka,

I am writing first to thank you for the lovely embroidered table cloth that you sent to me and my new husband Michael Dursa as a wedding present. I know you made it yourself, which makes it even more special. Our marriage vows were said before the priest in the town of New Salem this past July in St. Mary's Assumption Greek Catholic church there. It was a very simple ceremony, just the two of us and the priest.

We received your very, very sad news about the terrible diphtheria epidemic spreading over the Spiš region. And the news of the death of two of your young sons is more shocking: Little Janny, just 6 years old, dying in March, 1910, and Little Miško, just 3 years old, dying in December, 1910. I know you are not new to death. I remember your oldest son Jan, who died in 1909 at the age of 12 while we were visiting all of you in 1909, and your baby son Martin who died as an infant in 1901.

Our doctor here in Star Junction calls this diphtheria epidemic the "strangling angel of children." I call it the strangling <u>*devil, with the fever, sore throat, swollen glands, loss of appetite, and the extreme difficulty of breathing which leads to death.*</u>   The need for the black cross quarantine sign on houses that are affected only seems to attract the <u>*devil*</u>, in my opinion. We hear that the epidemic is worse in lower Hungary although there is word that a vaccine may be available to some doctors there soon. This is according to American doctors.

I have reread several times your letter and am especially saddened by your words explaining how young Miško died in the middle of winter with no one even available to build a coffin for the poor child. And how you and Martin decided to use your beloved hope chest as a coffin, and then you had to go by horse wagon up to the cemetery in Poráč to lay the child to rest in the middle of a snowstorm.

Katka, there is nothing more heartbreaking than the death of your own child. Please accept our prayers and hope that they can soothe your losses. I am praying for you and your parted children:
Hospodin je môj pastier; nebudem mať nedostatku (The Lord is my shepherd; I shall not want.
He maketh me to lie down in green pastures; He leadeth me beside the still waters.
Yea, though I walk through the valley of the shadow of death, I will fear no evil;
 for Thou art with me. I will dwell in the house of the Lord forever.)
From the 23rd Psalm.

With love from your sister & family in Star Junction,
Mária

Name: Joannes (Jan) Jurek
Birth: 04 Sep 1904, in Poráč, Spiš Slovakia
Death: 04 Mar 1910 in Rudňany, Spiš Slovakia

Name: Michal Jurek
Birth: 20 Dep 1907 in Poráč, Spiš Slovakia
Death: 06 Dec 1910 in Rudňany, Spiš Slovakia

Other samples can be viewed in *Slovenska L'udová Výšivka* (Slovak Folk Embroidery) by Anna Chlupová.

September 8, 1915, Star Junction, PA   *Všade dobre, doma najlepšie.* (There is no place like home.)

My dearest sister Katka,
We are so busy having babies that I must apologize for not writing sooner. Michael and I now have 2 Dursa girls: Veronika, born in 1911 and Julia born in 1913. That makes a dozen births for me, and according to my midwife: the end! Our sister Helen married Joseph Dursa on October 19, 1910 and she now also has two new babies: John born in 1911 and Mary born in 1913. Katie and John Duritsa, my daughter and son-in law, have 3 babies: George born in 1910, John born in 1912, and Anna born in 1914. So you see we are always busy. All of the newborns were baptized at St. Stephen's Church in Leisenring. Catharine Mrozko was the sponsor for all of the babies, and they all wore the same baptismal dress that Catharine brought with her from Poráč. As you know, our custom allows the godparents to take the baby to the church for the priest's baptism blessing. The parents remain home and prepare for the celebration. The first Sunday after the child's birth is usually the day of the baptism.

I am very lucky to still have Sophie at home for some of the time to help with the new girls and also help with the cooking and laundry for our own family and for the boarders who come mostly from Poráč. We cook them a decent breakfast in the morning, pack their lunches for their usual 12 hour work day, provide clean work clothes when they return, and of course serve them a decent supper. Just that is a full time job, not counting the same duties for our own family. We live in Michael Dursa's patch house in Star Junction, which is a two- bedroom half of a duplex. One bedroom upstairs is just for the boarders, and the second bedroom is for all of the girls: Sophie, Annie, Helen, Justina, Suzanna, all sleeping in the horizontal position on the double bed. The two young Dursa girls sleep downstairs in the living room with me and Michael, as do the boys Mike and Joe. So we are overloaded with adults and children. And, I am contantly giving stern warning to the girls to absolutely ignore any "funny business" coming from any of those male boarders who sleep upstairs.

We are called "The Star Junction Patch."   There are close to 77 Patches (nickname for "company town) in Fayette County today. A Patch is made up of rows and rows of nearly identical single or duplex houses; a company store where miners have an account (and it is expected that both the husband and wife will buy **all** of their daily needs from this store, not just food, but clothes, furniture, seeds, etc.); one or more churches (the money for the building of these is supplied by the mining company); a school, (the teacher (s) hired by the mining company); one doctor (maybe); and then the mine itself. The Connellsville Coke Region includes our Washington mine which contains the prized bituminous (soft) coal.   The H.C. Frick Coal Company makes any repairs to the houses and guarantees that the family has some land for vegetable and flower gardens and a place for perhaps a cow, a pig, or chickens. We have water at a neighborhood pump and a latrine shared with the other family in the adjoining duplex.

Usually the "Hunkies" (that is the slang word for mostly Slavic miners and their families who emigrated from the political state of Hungary) live within their own ethnic group, for language or religious purposes, so our neighbors have always been Slovaks. The Poles, Croats, Serbs, Slovenes, Russians, and Ukrainians live in their own clusters.

Both of my sons, Mike and Joe, are now employed in the mine. By the end of 4th grade they were ready to work and help out with family expenses, especially Joe, who for most of his school career was labeled a "trouble maker."   I don't know how many times the truant officer came to the house looking for Joe because he was not at school. Mike, on the other hand, was just the opposite and loved learning, especially the challenges of English. He would keep a homemade dictionary of English/Slovak so that he would not be embarrassed when I would send him to the company store. Naturally I would tell him what to buy, using the word in Slovak. When some customer in the store would give him the English word, he would write it down in his little homemade dictionary so he wouldn't be caught off guard again. Although there was no space or time to do any homework at home, he always received the highest marks in all subjects in school. I have to tell you, Katka, that when the children are all speaking English to each other, and I am understanding nothing, I just want to be back in Poráč and not have this terrible language problem. But instead of crying, I start yelling in Slovak at the children, *Prosím, počúvajte. Nehovorte doma po anglicky.* (Please, listen. Don't speak that English at home.) They look at me with fear and more often with hate. I cannot help then to feel guilty, knowing that I am causing a deep misunderstanding between them and me. It is then that I know how the streets are NOT made of gold in this land of Pennsylvania.

The boys each earn about 70 cents a day and the rent for our company house is $12.00 a month. Sophie works as a domestic 3 days a week for a Jewish family in Uniontown and stays at the Cohen's house overnight for those days. She contributes about $5.00 a month. She is able to come back and forth on the electric railway that connects the bigger towns in the Connellsville region.

The boys started working for the mine when they were 12 and 10 as "breaker boys." The coal that comes out of the mine is a mixture of coal, rock, slate and other junk called "culm." It is the job of the breaker boys to pick out the junk as the coal flows down the long iron chutes. The boys were not allowed to wear gloves, and it took several weeks for their hands to get hard enough to not feel pain from sorting this stuff. Finally, the clean coal continues on into railroad cars, ready for the coke ovens. The boys would come home covered with black coal dust. To keep from inhaling dust on the job, our boys wore handkerchiefs over their mouths and chewed wads of tobacco to keep their mouths moist. But I felt such sympathy for them every day when they returned home, filthy with black coal dust and sometimes wet from leaking rain where they had to work in an uncovered area.

Our brother Matej suffered a serious accident during work in the Washington mine. He was carried out of the mine by donkey driven coal car with a crushed back. The company doctor who attended him was not able to set his back correctly so poor Matej now cannot walk without the help of two canes, and of course he cannot work down in the mine any more but must supervise the breaker boys, or some other simpler and less paid job, so that he can at least give a little support for his family. His wife Annie must take in more boarders, having a day shift and a night shift of boarders, in order to put enough food on the table and pay the rent. *Bože môj. Bože môj.* (My God, My God). Sometimes life can be cruel.

We are thinking of all of you.
Your loving sister,
 Mária

Garden Patch, Star Junction, PA   Author's archive.

Coal Miners – Pennslyvania

Group of Miners, Drivers and Trapper, 1908.

Breaker boys, 1911.

Photos of Pennsylvania coal miners by Lewis W. Hine (1874-1940), courtesy of Library of Congress, Prints and Photographs Division, public domain, no known copyright restrictions.

Coal Miners' Children, Star Junction, PA (about 1912)

Helen Sirilla;   Steve Dursa;   Justina (Esther) Sirilla
(1903-2002)   (1902-1920)   (1905-1954) Pallo archive.

Post Office, Star Junction, PA   Author's photo.

December 1, 1918. Star Junction, PA   *Je to možné?*   (Is it possible?)

My dearest sister Katka,
Praise be to God and Jesus Christ. I have very, very sad news for you Katka. In November I buried two of my girls: Mária who died on November 11, 1918, and Anna who died one week later on November 18. Both were infected with the influenza virus which immediately turned into pneumonia. Also, my daughter Katie's baby, Stephen, died on November 23.

Mária was 27 years old and had been married since 1906, leaving her husband Ján Novák and five children. Her funeral was at St. Stephens Church with burial at the church's cemetery in Leisenring. Anna was 17 years old, just newly married and working as a maid in Uniontown. Her funeral was from St. John the Baptist Greek Catholic Church in Uniontown, and her burial was at St. John's cemetery in Hopwood. We were not even at her funeral and burial because her death was so sudden.

Both Mária and Anna were ill only a few days before they died, and people say that the ages most affected from this illness are from 20-40 years old. They say that this epidemic is the worst in world history, worse than the Black Death in the 1300s. Those affected are usually people who are exhausted, tired, and overworked.   That certainly explains why Mária and Anna became ill.

The mining company has issued strict precautions: avoid large groups of people (our church services have been cancelled for more than a month); wash hands frequently; do not share drinking cups and eating utensils.   The company store has offered extra eating and drinking utensils at no cost. Also we are supposed to wear a gauze mask when going outside, and these are also available at the company store at no cost. Because so many have already died, we hope we can stop this epidemic.

Some schools are closed, although ours in Star Junction is not. Our younger girls have come home with a very, very silly jump- rope song that they learned on the school playground:
  I had a little bird. Its name was Enza. I opened the window.   And in-flu-enza.

Katka, I don't think there is anything worse than the death of your own child, as you well know.   My heart aches for my two lovely girls, Mária and Anna. I hope that this epidemic does not reach Poráč. My praying over and over "Thy Will be Done." is my only consolation.
Hugs from your grieving sister, Mária.

Anna Sirilla (1901-1918)   **Mária Sirilla Novák (1891-1918)**

Author's archive.

December 6, 1918, Star Junction, PA   *Deň Svätého Mikuláša*   (St. Nicholas Day)

My dearest sister Katka,

Despite such a very sad November with the deaths of my two girls, Mária and Anna, and my daughter Katie's baby son, all from the terrible influenza epidemic, here we are today on one of our most beloved holidays, St. Nicholas Day. All of my Sirilla children are now grown up and beyond the interests of receiving gifts from St. Nicholas. My Sophie and Helen are now married; Michael still works in the mine; Joe has just returned from the army where he enlisted under an alias name and an exaggerated age, since I would not sign for him! (But all is forgiven now, I hope.)   Justina and Susanna work as maids in Perryopolis. My two Dursa girls, Vera and Julia, are now 7 and 5, so they will be putting their clean shoes and boots on the window sill so that St. Nicholas will fill them with candies and fruit when he visits during the night, knowing that they have been good children. Vera also wants to put some carrots and hay next to her shoes for St. Nicholas' horse. Their behavior has been extra "good" in the last few weeks because they do not want to receive a piece of coal in their shoes for "bad" behavior.

As you know, today is the anniversary of the death of the real bishop of Myra, St. Nicholas, who died in the 300s. There are many legends about him, but the one our children like the most is the one that says that on December 6th St. Nicholas climbs down to earth from heaven on a golden rope, and he is accompanied by an angel, his helper, and a devil who carries a whip and a bag of coal for those children who have misbehaved during the year.   Some of our children also believe that St. Nicholas comes down on a horse, so they put carrots and hay out for St. Nicholas' horse.

Here in Star Junction on December 6, it is popular for children to dress up as the bishop St. Nicholas, the angel, and the devil, and when the Sirilla children were young, Michael dressed as the bishop, Sophie was the angel, with a long white sheet over her body and her own hand crocheted crown on her head, and of course Joe was the devil, using his father's black overcoat and smearing black shoe polish over his face, carrying a bag of coal in his right hand, (As you know coal is not hard to find in Star Junction!) and ringing hand bells in his left hand.   (After 1909, Joe would wear the mask he brought back with him from Poráč.) The three would go to neighbors' homes here in the Patch where they knew there were young children and request that the little ones recite a prayer for them or perhaps sing a favorite song that they learned in church. Then the little ones would receive some candy or piece of fruit.   Should the little ones do nothing, then Joe, the devil, was ready to give each "bad" child a piece of coal! Or maybe two pieces! Some years a "dressed up" St. Nicholas would be at the Leisenring Company Store all day, along with an angel and a devil. The black-faced devil would usually scare the little ones to tears.

We usually made a special bread for this holiday in the form of the bishop's head, (*Biskupský Chelbiček*) which the children called *Chlieb Svätého Mikuláša* (Mr. Saint Nicholas' Bread). The child who made the eyes out of sugar balls and raisins and the beard out of salt kernels had the most fun. We used a standard sweet bread recipe, and of course everyone wanted to style the eyes and beard! So each year a different child was chosen for this job, but "taking turns" was not always a popular idea. With so many children in the family, I rarely had a chance to enjoy a single child one at a time, so this kind of group fun had to substitute.

Katka, how quickly time passes and children grow up and develop their own families. I am thinking of you on this holiday and hope that your girls will receive candy and fruit from your own Svätý Mikuláš.
Your loving sister,
Mária

December 22, 1918. Lemont, PA   *Vianoce s posolstvom pokoja a lásky.*
                                  (Christmas with its message of peace and love.)

My dearest sister Katka,

I am sending my family's greetings for Christmas, *Veselé Vianoce.* We are not like our usual happy selves awaiting this holiday time because of the terrible influenza epidemic that caused such grief for our family. So in two days we will have our Christmas Eve mass with special prayers for all members' deceased loved ones and especially for our dear Maria, Anna, and Baby Stephen. Each family is cooking their Slovak specialty and I chose *pirohý* for the Dursa family. The girls and I have been very busy for the past days with all of this cooking.

For our *Štedrý večer* (Christmas Eve) dinner, the girls and I will be cooking for two days in order to have out traditional foods for this special dinner which begins with the first star in the sky. We put our Slovak *Jasličky* (Manger scene) in the middle of the table. The figures are all made of straw, which is to remind all of us that the Holy Child, *Ježiško*, (Baby Jesus) was poor and bedded on straw.

My husband Michael will begin the meal with a prayer, reading from Luke 2:11:
"Today in the city of David there has been born for you a Savior, who is Christ the Lord."
Then he will follow with his best wish:
"On this glorious eve of the birthday of Christ our Lord, I wish you my family good health, happiness, and *many blessings."*

Then he will first come to my side and make a sign of the cross on my forehead with honey and say:
"Dearest wife, tonight is your one night of the year free of serving our meal. I will serve for you tonight, and you may sit with the children and enjoy all of your cooking. May the love between us stay as sweet as this honey." Then I will make a sign of the cross on each child's forehead with the honey and sometimes add garlic and say, *"May you always love your parents as sweetly as this honey."*

The meal begins with the *oplátký* (wafers), which we buy from the priest at our church. Each person receives a wafer, much like the communion in the church. We ask the children to recite together the grace before the meal: *"Bless us Oh Lord and these thy gifts, which we are about to receive from Thy bounty, through Christ our Lord, Amen."*

The next course is the appetizer, which is the favored *bobál'ky* (the round biscuits dipped in honey and poppy seed). Next is the *kapustnica* (sauerkraut soup) followed by the *ryba* (fried carp). We purchase a live fish at the company store, put it in a bucket, and keep it fresh until December 24 when Michael prepares it for the cooking. Along with the fish course comes our own recipe for potato salad and pea salad. This is followed by *pirohý*, the small dough squares filled with cheese and potatoes. Usually the sound of a tinkling bell is heard next, made by the Baby Jesus, announcing time for small gift openings next to our small pine tree that we hang from the ceiling and decorate with gingerbread cookies, small apples, and candles. After the gifts, it is time for our favorite desserts: *orechovník* (walnut roll) and *mákovník* (poppy seed roll). Then a sample of *slivovica* (plum brandy) is popular for the adults. The evening closes with the singing of our favorite carol, *Tichá noc* (Silent Night).

Katka, you see we will have the same foods that you will have at your Christmas Eve dinner in Rudňany. May we all have health and courage to face any hardship in the New Year, 1919. *Veselé Vianoce a Radostný Nový Rok* (Merry Christmas and a Happy New Year) for you and your family.

Your loving sister, Mária

Original church: Abt 1910.

Original iconostas: Abt 1910.

January 22, 1919. Star Junction, PA   *Ked' sa chce, tak sa dá .* (Where there's a will, there's a way.)

My dearest sister Katka,

I am sending greetings for a Happy New Year. We are still <u>not</u> like our usual happy selves at this time of year because of the terrible influenza epidemic that caused such grief in our family. The memorial mass in Leisenring for all the deceased loved ones was said by the Rev. Zubricky on Christmas Eve, and I can now say that I have a better peace of mind.

We are very proud that our church was the first church in this area of southwestern Pennsylvania of the Greek Catholic faith. Of course most of the adults of our family will never forget our dear *Svätý Demetrius Kostol* in Poráč.

You might wonder how our church was founded. In 1892 Rev. Alexander Dzubay came to this area to assist our people in forming a church. Leisenring was selected as a central site in Fayette County.   The H.C. Frick Coal & Coke Company donated the ground, approximately 12 acres and still makes a monthly donation to the church.   Over 70 communities are served, and our extended families live in some of the following towns that serve this church: Perryopolis, Star Junction, Vanderbilt, Dawson, Connellsville, Dunbar, Lemont, Uniontown, Redstone, Leisenring, New Salem, Brownfield.   At first there was no public transportation, so we all **walked** many miles to church every Sunday. Now there is an electric rail service built by the H. C. Frick Coke Company connecting most of the towns, so it is much easier to attend church services and social events in Leisenring. I always put aside a little money from selling eggs so that we always have a small donation for the church every Sunday.

Katka, I forgot to mention in my last letter anything about your very special new holiday, October 28, 1918, the official day of the new country of Czecho-Slovakia, uniting the Czechs and Slovaks. We here in Pennsylvania read our Slovak newspaper *Amerikánsko Slovenské Noviny,* printed in Pittsburgh. So October 28, 1918, your first national holiday, slipped by us here, but I must say that this new union must fall on blessed ears for all Slovaks. After 1,000 years of domination by Hungarians, Slovakia will no longer be the Hungarian "felvidék" (pronounced felveedake) the highlands.   The Tatra Mountains now belong to the Slovaks. I hope we will never again hear the Hungarian chant, *Tót nem ember*, (Tót pronounced tote) meaning "a Slovak is not a person."

Mám rád moju novu krajinu, Česko-Slovensko. (I love my new country called Czecho-Slovakia.) We all hope that this new dream will last forever.   Czechs and Slovaks have been brothers forever.

Katka give our hugs to all for a very *Radostný Nový Rok,* (Happy New Year). *Do nového roka prajem všetkým št'astie a lásku. (*For the new year, I wish everyone happiness and love.)

Your loving sister,
Mária

Family Group Sheet for Elias (Eli) Durica (Dyuritza)

Husband:	Elias (Eli) Durica (Dyuritza)
Birth:	01 Aug 1879 in Porac, (Spis) Slovakia
Death:	12 Aug 1919 in Star Junction, PA, Bur. St.Stephen's Byz.Cem. Leisenring PA
Marriage:	1900 in Connellsville, Fayette, Pennsylvania, USA
Father:	Michal Durica
Mother:	Maria Mrozko

Wife:	Helena Nemcsik(Nemchik)
Birth:	06 Sep 1880 in Porac, (Spis) Slovakia
Death:	30 May 1916 in Fergus Falls, Otter Tail County, Minnesota
Father:	Joannes Nemcsik
Mother:	Maria Szivacsko

Children:

1 F	Name:	Julia Josephine Duritza
	Birth:	03 Mar 1910 in Browerville, Todd, Minnesota, USA
	Death:	18 Sep 1994 in Eastpointe, (Macomb) , Michigan

2 F	Name:	Esther J Duritza
	Birth:	11 Jun 1912 in Browerville, Todd, Minnesota, USA
	Death:	10 Jul 2000 in Huntington Beach, Orange, California, USA
	Spouse:	Emil J Geyer

3 M	Name:	Michael Duritza
	Birth:	04 Nov 1915 in Browerville, Todd, Minnesota, USA
	Death:	24 Mar 2001 in McKeesport, Allegheny, Pennsylvania, USA
	Spouse:	Helen Elko

Orphaned Children of Eliáš Dyuritza:
Julia; Michael; Esther
(Abt 1917), Š. Cvengroš archive.

August 18, 1919 Star Junction, PA   *Nič sa nedari.* *(*Nothing is going right.)

My dearest sister Katka:
I hope this letter finds you enjoying the summer. Here in Star Junction we buried our brother Eliáš,
who died on August 12 of what the doctor called tuberculosis, but Michael and I feel that maybe
Eliáš had been infected with the influenza (Spanish flu) virus, and that that was the cause of death.
There is more to this tragedy. Eliáš' wife, Helena Nemscik, died in 1916 (only a few months after their
third child, Michael, was born,) in Fergus Falls, Minnesota after being admitted to the mental hospital of
Otter Tail County. Eliáš, along with his wife's brother, who had a farm right next to his (and not far from
John Shrilla's farm), told the children that their mother was killed in a car accident to make the loss a
little easier for the girls. Naturally, little Michael was too young to understand. Katka, like you, Eliáš'
wife Helen lost 4 children as infants. It's no wonder that she suffered from depression.   Now with the
death of Eliáš , their father, the three living children are left as orphans, and they are still in shock over
this tragedy of the loss of both parents. *Bože môj. Bože môj.* (My God, My God.)

Our brother John Duritza was named guardian of the children in Eliáš' will. Eliáš left the money from
the sale of his farm in Browerville, Minnesota to his children naturally. Our brother John will have to go
through probate court in Todd County, Minnesota and in Fayette County, Pennsylvania to get the
custody and money arrangements legalized.

I am enclosing a photo of the children, taken probably in 1917 before Eliáš and the children left
Browerville and came here to Star Junction where Eliáš was able to return to his coal mining job.

I will tell you what I know about the move to Browerville, Minnesota:
In about 1905 my brother-in-law, Ján Sirilla (John Shirilla), heard about cheap land available in
Minnesota from several Polish coal miners. These miners had relatives who had purchased farm land
in Todd County near Browerville, which is northwest of Minneapolis.   Advertisements stated that this
area had the most fertile and cheap farm land available in all of Minnesota. Eliáš was impressed with
these stories, and you remember how his namesake, Mama's brother Eliáš Mrozko, always told him
that the best job in life was being a farmer. When our brother Eliáš left Poráč in 1895, he told me (you
remember that I and my two girls were still living with Mama) that his dream, when he saved enough
money from coal mining jobs in Fayette County, was to buy land somewhere and farm. It was in 1896
that my husband Michal came back to Poráč and we decided to all return to Ohio. You probably
remember that it was Ján Sirila, Michal's brother, who accompanied me on the ship and helped me with
the two girls. Both Eliáš and Ján knew each other from school life in Poráč, as you remember.

So when my brother-in-law John (Ján) said "Let's go to Minnesota with the Polish guys." Eliáš was
more than happy to see this faraway Minnesota for himself. Both of them bought 40 acre plots of land
near each other on Route #4. The area eventually had about 20 families of the Greek Catholic faith and
both Eliáš and John were founding members of Holy Trinity Greek Catholic Church (1913) located east of
Browerville on a hill near the Long Prairie River.

Katka, in addition to the photo of Eliáš' children, I am enclosing a photo of John Shirilla's barn where he
housed his cows and sold his milk to a dairy in Browerville. Eliáš concentrated on raising grain: wheat
and rye. I wish you were here with us to help console us during this mourning for the loss of our dear
brother. My heart is heavy with sadness.

Your loving sister, Mária

Browerville, Minnesota

John Shirilla's Barn and Photo (far right), 1939. Author's archive.

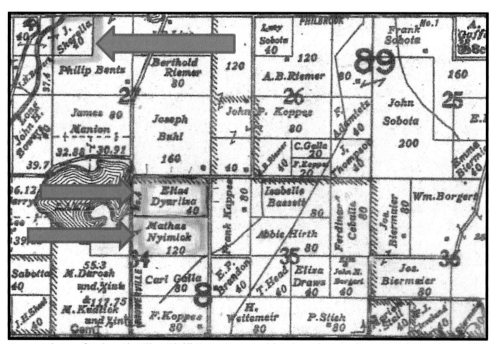

Farm plots of John Shirilla, Eliáš Dyuritza and his brother-in-law Mathias Nymscik.
State: Minnesota; County: Todd; Town: Ward; Year: 1914.
U.S. Indexed County Land Ownership Maps, 1860-1918 Courtesy of Minnesota
Historical Society, St. Paul, MN 2016.

Will of Elias Dyuritza, Deceased.

I, Elias Dyuritza, of Star Junction County of Fayette and State of Penn. being of sound mind, and memory and understanding, do make and publish this _____ my last Will and Testament, hereby revoking and making void all former Wills by me at any time heretofore made.

1st I will and bequeath to my three children, Julia Dyuritza, Josephine Dyuritza and Michael Dyuritza my farm consisting of One Hundred Three and one half Acres situated in Todd County, Minnesota, Same being part of _____

2d. Be it _____ _____ to John Foist of Browerville, _____ _____ Four Thousand Five Hundred Do_____ _____ (Fifteen Hundred Dollars) on this farm. Ther_____ $400.00. Mr. Foist also assumes Foist agreed to pay $200.00 pe_____ pay 6 % interest on Back payme_____

3rd. I will a_____ _____ consisting of $1000.00 be us_____ _____ three children after my funer_____ _____ is paid.

4th I will t_____ _____ halluciationless _____ payments on_____ for my three children and a_____ _____ after my demise, and _____ _____ until they become of age

6th I will ou_____ Dyuritza, $1000.00 cash _____ to be used toward the su_____ my _____ my sisters, Mrs. Mary D_____

I do hereby _____ Dyuritza of Star Junction_____ I will and Testament.

In Witness whereof, I, Elias Dyuritza, the testator above named, have hereunto subscribed my name and affixed my seal the 23rd day of June, in the year of our Lord one thousand nine hundred Nineteen

Elias Dyuritza (Seal).

Signed, sealed, published and delivered by the above named Elias Dyuritza as and for his last Will and Testament, in the presence of us, who have hereunto subscribed our names at his request as witnesses thereto in the presence of the said Testator and of each other

Edmund Morton
Mike Sirilla

Courtesy of the Minnesota Historical Society, 2016.

CERTIFICATE OF DEATH

COMMONWEALTH OF PENNSYLVANIA
DEPARTMENT OF HEALTH
BUREAU OF VITAL STATISTICS

1. PLACE OF DEATH.

County of _Fayette_

Township of _Perry_

or
Borough of _____

or
City of _____ (No. _____ St., Ward.)

Registration District No. _2571_

Primary Registration District No. _____

File No. _71192_

Registered No. _42_

[If death occurred in a Hospital or institution, give its NAME instead of street and number.]

2. FULL NAME _Steve Dursa_

PERSONAL AND STATISTICAL PARTICULARS	MEDICAL CERTIFICATE OF DEATH

3. SEX _M_

4. COLOR OR RACE _W_

5. SINGLE, MARRIED, WIDOWED OR DIVORCED (Write the word.) _Single_

6. DATE OF BIRTH _Aug 31 1902_ (Month) (Day) (Year)

7. AGE _18 9 16_

IF LESS than 1 day how many.........hrs. or

16. DATE OF DEATH _Jun 16 1920_ (Month) (Day) (Year)

17. I HEREBY CERTIFY, That I attended deceased from ___191__, to ___191__,

that I last saw h___ alive on ___191__,

and that death occurred, on the date stated above, at _4 30_ M.

The CAUSE OF DEATH was as follows:

Gun Shot Wound of Leg.
Severing Femoral Artery
probably Homicide

(Duration) ___ yrs. ___ mos. ___ ds.

Contributory (Secondary) _182_

(Duration) ___ yrs. ___ mos. ___ ds.

(Signed) _Jno Blair Dept Coroner_

Uniontown, _Morning Herald_
Thursday, June 17, 1920

YOUTH DIES FROM GUNSHOT WOUND

Echard Works Youth Wounded Accidentally, It Is Believed. Coroner Notified.

Loss of blood from a gunshot wound sustained, accidentally, it is believed, 10 hours previous caused the death Wednesday morning of Steve Dursa, aged 18, at the home of his parents, Mr. and Mrs. Mike Dursa at Echard works near Star Junction. Dursa and John Puzak, in company with some other boys, were walking along the road with linked arms, when the accident occurred. Puzak, it is said, exhibiting a revolver which is reported to have been accidentally discharged.

The members of the party in which also were Steve Sobodash and Charles Boon, carried Dursa to his home a short distance away. Efforts to stop the flow of blood from the wound in his leg proved futile and he died from loss of blood Wednesday morning. Puzak after the shooting is said to have thrown the revolver into the reservoir and to have disappeared after helping the injured youth home.

Facts in the case were reported to Coroner S. H. Baum yesterday and he has made arrangements to go to Echard works today to investigate the shooting which has not been explained entirely satisfactorily to officials. Funeral services for the victim will be held Friday morning at 9:30 o'clock followed by interment in the Leisenring cemetery.

Uniontown, _Morning Herald_
September 8, 1921

Upon binding instructions of Judge J. Q. Van Swearingen, the jury returned a verdict of not guilty in the case of John Puzak, charged with the murder of Steve Dursa at Star Junction on June 15, 1920. It developed from the testimony that the defendant, the deceased and two other young men started out on the evening of the shooting for a walk, walking two abreast and the deceased in the rear of the defendant.

As they were walking through a field a shot was fired and turning the defendant saw the gun drop from the hands of the deceased. None of the party saw him handling the gun and presumed that he was playing with it when it exploded. Picking the gun up the defendant threw it over into a reservoir adding that "this gun will never shoot anybody else." Inasmuch as he had picked the gun up suspicion rested on him and upon advice of a friend he made his escape and was arrested at Newport, R. I., being enlisted in the naval service. At the time of the shooting Puzak was but 15 years of age and the deceased 17.

Death of Steve Dursa. Courtesy of http://www.chroniclingamerica.loc.gov

June 18, 1920 Star Junction, PA   *Ako Pán žiada, tak to bude.*   (As the Lord wills, so it shall be.)

My dearest sister Katka,
We have been back home in our patch house here in Star Junction just a few hours. We buried my husband's son, Steve Dursa, in the Leisenring Cemetery after a mass at St. Stephen's Church. Steve would have been 19 years old at his upcoming birthday in August and was such a handsome young man.

Steve was walking home from the mine with three of his friends. He was carrying a loaded pistol of one of these friends in the pocket of his right pants when the gun went off accidentally and the bullet lodged into the femoral artery in his right leg.   The boys quickly carried him to our home, and he was bleeding badly. We tried contacting the patch doctor, but we had no luck, so we did our best to contain the bleeding.   Steve died 6 hours later.

Katka, I can't tell you how overcome with grief is Michael. Steve was his only living child. And he lost his wife in 1907 after only 6 years of marriage. She too is buried in Leisenring.   This was an awful shock watching such a young person die, and the burial in Leisenring caused me to relive my first husband, Michael's death in 1908 and of course to revisit his grave in this cemetery. I also relived my first daughter's death of influenza in 1918, just two years ago, and I had to visit her gravesite too.   It has been a very, very sad day.

Most of my children were at the mass and burial for Steve: Katie and her family, Sophie and her family, my son Mike, and the four younger daughters: Justina, Susanna, Vera, and Julia. My son Joe was away in the Army, and daughter Helen is now living in Chicago.   Also our sister Helen and her husband Joe Dursa and their children came from Uniontown. Helen's husband, Joe, was an uncle to young Steve.

Every time I am at this cemetery in Leisenring, I can't help but be so homesick for Poráč. The rolling hills and the views are so similar to our homeland. I wish you were here to help console all of us.

Your loving sister,
Mária

St. Stephen's Greek Catholic Church & Cemetery, Leisenring, PA Author's photo.

COUSINS

*Esther Dyuritza & Helen Duritza at John Duritza's
farm, Herbert, PA (Abt 1922). M. Peel archive.*

*Esther Sirilla, Julia Dyuritza, Sue Sirilla
Star Junction, PA (Abt 1920). Š. Cvengroš archive.*

July 11, 1922, Star Junction, PA   *Ked prši tak leje.*   (When it rains, it pours.)

My dearest sister Katka,

I have again sad news to tell you. Sister Anna's husband, Joseph Sopkovich II, died today in Youngstown and will be buried in the cemetery of St. Mary's Church in Youngstown. He suffered for a long time with stomach problems.   You probably don't remember that he was born in Koterbachy in 1860, not far from where you live now at #261. Mother Mrozko knew the Sopkovich family and arranged the marriage for Anna which occurred January 7, 1892 in St. Vincent's Abbey, Latrobe, Pennsylvania. That is one reason she accompanied me on my voyage from Poráč to Hubbard, Ohio in 1891. Since Joseph worked in the mines near Brownfield, they lived there after their marriage. They moved to Youngstown about one year after their third child, Michael, was born in 1899 and bought a confectionary store at 503 Steel Street. The other son Nicholas was born in Youngstown in 1909. Helen, Julia, and Paul all died as infants. Poor Anna, what a heartbreak to lose her wonderful husband, Joseph.

I also have to tell you that Julia Dyuritza, the oldest daughter of our brother Eliáš, is not well; she slips into deep depression frequently and becomes silent to the rest of the world. Of the three children left orphans by the tragic death of their mother and later the terrible illness and death of their father, Julia seems the most affected. She came to us in 1920. I volunteered to take in Julia because she became very attached to my daughters, Justina and Susanna. Our brother John agreed to continue to keep the two other children: Esther and Miško.

Because the coal mines in Fayette County are soon closing, and with that the jobs ending, my Michael feels that working in the steel mills in Youngstown would be a good job opportunity. Our brother John is planning to move to Youngstown and according to John, the steel workers are the best paid of all workers in the United States because of the strong steel workers union. The owners of the coal mines think that the United Mine Workers Union is run by communists, and the bosses think just because our men and boys do not speak good English, that they can be treated like dogs.

The last time we visited Anna and her family in Youngstown, I was shocked to see the sky aglow with flames from the mills and the clouds of smoke bellowing out of the smokestacks. The acid smell of the sulfur in the air made me feel like throwing up. Please, dear God, is this better than the pollution of Fayette county?

But Katka, we have found a house to buy in Youngstown, and the house comes with a corner vacant lot. We can live in the basement of 718 Steel St. and rent the 1st floor to a family and also rent the 2nd floor. With this savings and whatever we can scrape up, we can build a house for us on the vacant lot. We can get house plans from the Sears Catalog and hope we can get some relatives to work on the framing. Michael is a very good concrete layer, so he will be able to do the foundation, of course with help. Our son Joe is now home from the Army and knows enough about carpentry that he wants to work on the framing along with Anna's son Stephen. Well, Katka it will be a city house, but of course we will have a garden area for vegetables and grapes and a coop for some chickens and I hope some geese. And speaking of geese, I will miss our flock and all of the wonderful pillows and quilts we have made from those beautiful feathers. However, no child has ever told me, "Mama, I just love stripping feathers!" or " Mama, I just love walking in your geese's poop all over the yard while the gander is hissing his tongue out at me!" But every child has always said, "I just love my down pillow and my feather quilt *(perina)*!"

Just yesterday as I was shopping at the general store in Leisenring , I saw the most unusual and beautiful display on the bulletin board of geese, drawn and colored by the 5th graders at the local primary school. The geese just came alive, and I had tears in my eyes thinking of having to sell or give away our flock when we move to Youngstown.   My dream has always been that if I had to stay in Ameryka, then I wanted to save and save and save money so that my husband and I could buy a farm, not as big as the one our brother John has in Herbert, PA, but a few acres and away from the Patch and the mines.

Well Katka, we will not have a farm but a house in the city! However, we will have running water, an indoor toilet, street cars, and plenty of neighbors.   I hope we like it. The 5 girls will of course move with us and already we have domestic jobs for the 3 older girls; the two younger Dursa girls will still be in school.   Everyday I am getting told by the older girls, "We do not want you to 'match' us with a husband. In America, girls and boys select each other for marriage based on 'love'!" My four oldest daughters, Maria, Katharina, Sophie, and Helen, were all matched to young men born in Slovakia, and are they so unhappy? I don't think so. I can still remember my "matched" marriage to Michal Širila. I barely knew him before we were standing next to each other at the front of St. Demetrius Church in Poráč. I knew about him from aunts, and since I was the oldest girl in the family, I had to obey my parents' choice for a marriage partner. Well, in hindsight, Katka, maybe I never knew about "love," just obedience and hard work. I don't always like the new customs of Ameryka, but maybe this one of "falling in love" is an improvement, although I would never admit it to the girls.

Katka, I have more surprises. My son Joe bought himself a car using his departure money from the Army! It's a 1921 Ford, so he will <u>drive</u> us to Youngstown for the funeral of Joseph, Anna's husband. This will be my first time as a passenger in a car! *Ježiš, Mária*, I am not looking forward to the trip, but we must go and comfort our sister during this hard time.

Katka, I am sending love and hugs to you and your family. My next letter will be from Youngstown. Your loving sister, Mária

John Duritza & Sons
M. Peel archive.

Left to right
Mike, Bill, Tom, Father John,
Paul, John

Father John (Maria's brother)
was naturalized in 1907.
He was 5'11", brown eyes,
brown hair.

Family Group Sheet for Jan (John) Durica

Husband:		Jan (John) Durica
	Birth:	23 May 1885 in Porac, (Spis) Slovakia
	Death:	09 Jun 1969 in Tuscon, AZ Bur.St.Nicholas Cem.,Campbell,OH
	Marriage:	04 Feb 1905 in New Salem, Fayette, Pennsylvania, USA
	Father:	Michal Durica
	Mother:	Maria Mrozko

Wife:		Katherine Varmega
	Birth:	Abt. 1888 in Porac, (Spis) Slovakia
	Death:	11 Oct 1977 in Detroit, Wayne, Michigan, USA
	Father:	
	Mother:	

Children:

1 F	Name:	Mary Duritza
	Birth:	1906 in Pennsylvania

2 M	Name:	Steve Duritza
	Birth:	Abt. 1908 in Pennsylvania

3 F	Name:	Katherine Duritza
	Birth:	17 Dec 1909 in Fayette County, Pennsylvania, USA
	Death:	08 Nov 2002 in Fullerton, Orange, California, USA
	Marriage:	1927
	Spouse:	Anthony Husic

4 F	Name:	Anna Duritza
	Birth:	1911 in Fayette County, Pennsylvania, USA
	Death:	Gross Point , Michigan

5 F	Name:	Helen Duritza
	Birth:	11 Jun 1912 in Fayette County, Pennsylvania, USA
	Death:	05 Jun 2007 in Fullerton, Orange, California, USA
	Spouse:	John Steffen

6 M	Name:	John Duritza
	Birth:	Abt. 1917 in Pennsylvania

7 M	Name:	Mike Duritza
	Birth:	Abt. 1918 in Pennsylvania

8 F	Name:	Elizabeth Duritza
	Birth:	Abt. 1921 in Pennsylvania

9 F	Name:	Eleanor Duritza
	Birth:	Abt. 1923 in Ohio

10 M	Name:	Paul Duritza
	Birth:	01 Jul 1927 in Ohio
	Death:	23 Jul 1987 in Youngstown, Mahoning, Ohio

11 M	Name:	William Duritza
	Birth:	09 Jun 1929 in Ohio
	Death:	19 Sep 1956

12 M	Name:	Thomas Duritza
	Birth:	Abt. 1932 in Ohio

Joseph Sopkovich with son Stefan. Brownfield, PA (Abt 1905).
Š. Cvengroš archive.

Joseph Sopkovich Death Certificate, dated July 11, 1922.

PART THREE – YOUNGSTOWN, OHIO

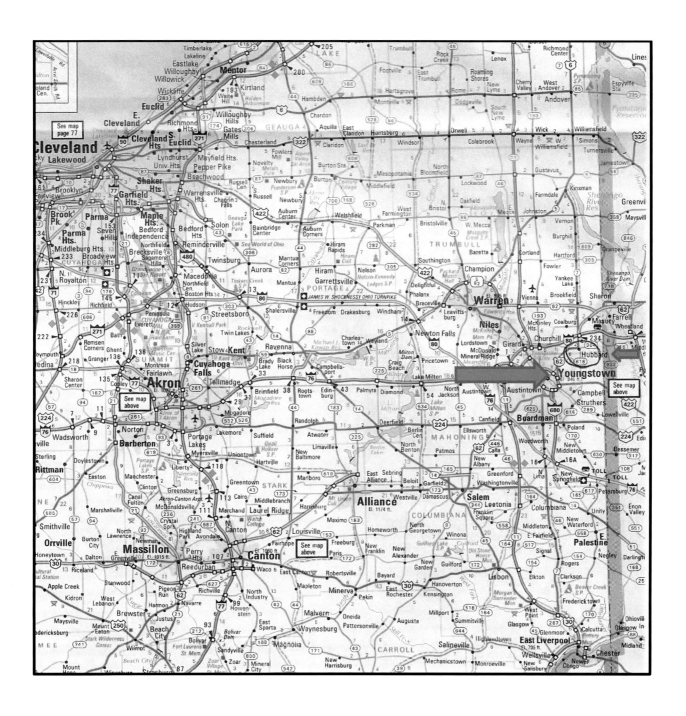

Youngstown

718 and 722 Steel Street, Youngstown, OH (Abt 1925). Š. Cvengroš archive.

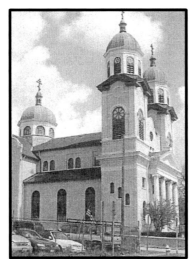

St. Nicholas Greek Catholic Church,
Dedicated 1919. Author's archive.

St. Mary's Greek Catholic Church.
Dedicated 1900. Author's archive.

July 1, 1923 Youngstown, OH   *Mám sa dobre.   A budem sa mat' ešte lepšie.*
(I am fine, and I'll be even better later.)

My dearest sister Katka,

We are now in Youngstown, living at 718 Steel Street, in the basement, having rented the first and second floors to families we knew in Poráč. We have contracted with Steve Sopkovich, son of sister Anna, to build our house on the empty corner lot of Steel and Butler Streets. The address will be 722 Steel Street. My son Joe will also work as a carpenter, helping Steve, and it will probably take a year to complete the plans that we ordered from last year's Sears catalog. I am drawing a copy of the blueprints to send you.   This Sears company sells everything for the home and farm, and you order from a huge book based on just the pictures. They also sell house plans.

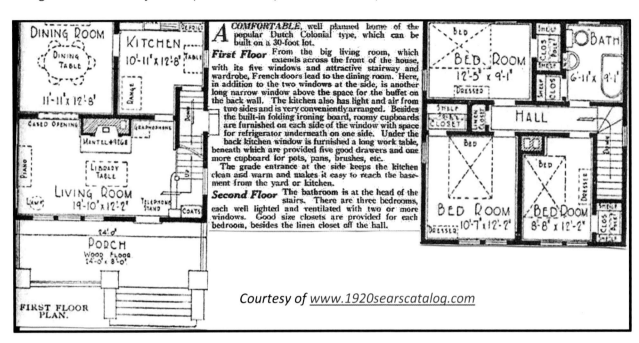

Courtesy of www.1920searscatalog.com

We will make a few changes to these plans. The front door will open into an entry room that will lead into the kitchen. A double door on the left of this entry room will lead into the living room and the dining room. The stairway to the second floor will remain to the very right, and the stairway down to the basement will be accessible from the kitchen with access also to the yard, making it easy to bring in vegetables and fruit from the garden.

Upstairs, we will put all five girls in one bedroom, 2 men boarders in bedroom #2, and 2 or 3 boarders in the larger bedroom #3. Michael and I will sleep in the downstairs living room. In the attic I will eventually have my loom for rag rug weaving, (with access from the second floor) but for now the two person loom will be in the basement where we will also have a washing machine, a furnace, and a cellar for storing vegetables and fruit in the winter. And of course there will be plenty of space for wine and slivovice making in the fall. It feels like we will be living in a castle, or more like moving to Spišský hrad with all of this space!

So this is the beginning of making our "dreams can come true." Our youngest daughters will live in a beautiful house and go to good schools in Youngstown, far away from the hardships of the Patch, the putrid air, and the endless dust from the coal mines. Of course we will miss our daughters Katie and

Sophie and their families, still living in Fayette County. Michael my husband will be employed with Youngstown Ice Company, where he will not have to work at the furnaces that make the steel.

Katka, I am sending my greetings to you and your family and hope that your summer is very pleasant.
Your loving sister,
Mária

Oh, by the way I'm sending you this postcard of the Republic Iron and Steel Works in Youngstown.

General View of the Republic Iron and
Steel Works, Youngstown, Ohio.

Courtesy of www.familyoldphotos.com Abt 1920.

A popular saying in Youngstown was:

"Everybody breathing dirt, eating dirt, they call it 'pay dirt,'
For if Youngstown were <u>clean</u>,
It would be Youngstown <u>out of work</u>."

August 1, 1924 Youngstown, OH   *Čas všetko vylieči.* (Time is a great healer.)

My dearest sister Katka,
We are now into our second summer in the hot sulfur-laden air of Youngstown as hundreds of pounds of molten steel are being made in the ovens of Carnegie's steel mills. Sometimes it seems like we left one pollution for another.   It is easily 100 degrees F. or higher now in the summer.   Men work long shifts. Michael works for Youngstown Ice Company and our brother John works for Republic Steel Company.

Our new house is not yet finished, but soon the kitchen and main living areas will be finished and we will move into that space while we finish the upstairs during the winter.   Michael, son Joe, and nephew Steve Sopkovich are working practically day and night. When they finish, Joe will return to Pennsylvania because he is engaged to marry a young Slovak woman named Catharine Dzurilla, born in Spišský Hrhov, not far from Poráč in Spiš, and she lives with her family in Vanderbilt.

My daughter Justina has decided to change her name to "Esther." She found in a book of Slovak name days that "Estera" name day was only 2 days before "Justina" in April. She thinks "Esther" sounds more American, and now she will be Esther Justine! Susanna wants to be "Susie" or "Susan," which she says is also more American. *Ježiš Mária, nerozumiem.* (I don't understand.)

I often hear Esther and Sue whispering something about their sister Helen in Chicago. I hope they are not getting any ideas about leaving Youngstown for Chicago. Their sister Helen says she needs help caring for her two children while she works as a seamstress in a factory that makes ladies' underwear. Her husband, Alex, a musician, does not have a steady job.   Esther and Sue work for nice families who live "on the hill" in Youngstown. They are able to live with the families during the week, and at the end of the week give us their pay checks. They tell me that "giving your parents your paycheck is also **not** very American."   Helen writes them about good jobs in Chicago, and Helen says that the pay check stays with the owner and does not go to the parent!

Julia, our brother Eliáš' orphaned daughter, has been diagnosed by a psychiatrist here in Youngstown as "severe depression due to grief." She works as a maid for a family on the west side of Youngstown, and the wife in the family says that she hears Julia often crying in her room, saying, "Dear God, take me off this earth." The psychiatrist feels that the loss of both of her parents, especially her mother at an early age, is the basis of the problem.   I have talked to our priest at St. Mary's Church, and his advice is to do what is best for Julia. I feel Julia needs medical help. I have spoken with brother John and Julia's sister Esther, who still lives with John and his family, and both of them feel we must do what is best for Julia. It's a hard decision because it would mean committing her to a mental hospital.   I know that time can be a great healer, but sometimes time alone is never enough.

Katka, having electricity, running water, paved streets and sidewalks, trolley cars, many Poráč Slovaks here as neighbors, in addition to being near sister Anna, brother John, brother Michael and all of their families, is like going to heaven. If only we didn't have the heavy responsibility of our niece Julia.

Give our love and greetings to your family and tell us what is new in Rudňany.

Your loving sister,
Mária

Chicago

State and Madison, Downtown Chicago, 1927
Courtesy of www.WBEZ.org
"The Great Years of Chicago's Streetcars" posted
Oct. 3, 2012 from WBEZ's blog.

Sisters: Justina (Esther) Sirilla & Susanna (Sue)
Sirilla. Chicago, IL (Abt 1925). Pallo archive.

August 1, 1925 Youngstown OH   *Aká matka, taká Katka.* (Like mother, like daughter.)

My dearest sister Katka,
We are now settled in the new house at 722 Steel St. in Youngstown. There is still much work left to do to get the house really finished, but we are all enjoying the lovely newness of the house and of course all of the conveniences. We are also happy to meet many people living in Youngstown who are originally from Poráč, as I told you in the last letter.

But now I will tell you all of the recent happenings to my family:

On 20 October, 1923, my son Michael married Helen Sohanage of Vanderbilt, PA. They were married in St. Nicholas Greek Catholic Church in Perryopolis. Then they moved in with her parents in Vanderbilt.

On 24 June, 1925, my son Joseph married Catharine Dzurilla, also of Vanderbilt, at St. Nicholas Church in Perryopolis. Then they too moved in with her parents in Vanderbilt.

In the fall of 1925, Sophie and her family moved to Yonkers, NY where her husband, Andy, had a brother, John Kuchta, who encouraged them to buy a grocery store at 143 Stanley Ave. in Yonkers. Sophie was so happy to leave Fayette County and have Andy away from the coal mines and the unions. Their 5 children of course moved with them.

Also in the fall of 1925, my two daughters Justina (Esther) and Susanna (Sue) left Youngstown for Chicago! As I wrote you last time, they had been talking about this trip for many months since their sister Helen was already living in Chicago for several years. They told me, "Mama, we are only going to visit." Yes I know what that means. I too told our mother in Poráč the same thing, "I am only going to America to visit!" And look at me now, almost 30 years have passed so quickly! Of course I was heartbroken for Justina and Susanna to leave, but all I could say is "You can always come back." They think there are factory jobs in Chicago with good pay, better than working as a maid in Youngstown, and also Helen says she needs help with her two children. *Budeme vidiet.* (We'll see.)

Our brother John Duritza asked me if I would take in the youngest of Eliáš' children, Miško, who is now almost 10 years old, and of course I said yes. John is raising 5 of his own boys along with 5 girls and brother Eliáš 'orphaned daughter, Esther. So now we have Vera and Julia Dursa and Miško Dyuritza who are all in school.

Katka, I hope that this letter finds you and your family enjoying a nice summer in Rudňany.
Your loving sister,
Mária

Tetka Mária (Aunt Maria)
Synovec Miško (Nephew Mikey)
Abt 1925.
Author's archive.

Slovak Rag Rugs

Mária Fabianová Širillová, Poráč, 1990 with her handričkova tkáčka (handwoven rag rug). Other Slovak rugs pictured are from family and friends.
Author's photo.

October 29, 1929 Youngstown, OH   *Dobrý deň. Možeš mi dat' peniaze?*
                                    (Hello. Brother can you spare a dime?)

My dearest sister Katka,

I am listening to a Slovak radio program coming from a Youngstown studio, and I don't really understand today's news: banks and the stock market have crashed! The announcer says to go to your bank as soon as possible tomorrow and withdraw all of your money. Maybe Michael will be able to explain it to me when he comes home. Already his total number of hours at work have been shortened. Katka, I think this might mean big trouble for jobs.

I have been weaving rag rugs on a loom similar to the one we used in Poráč. It requires at least two people, one to pass the weft through the warp and another person to beat the weft down. So I have the loom strung in the basement and my daughter Vera is my helper.   But now that Michael is not working 40 plus hours a week, he is building me a sit down "American style" loom in the attic. Now I know it will be extra hot in summer in the attic, but most of the weaving is done in the winter, so I think the attic will be a wonderful place to work. I have been selling my rugs at St. Mary's Church's holiday bazaars, and I'm trying to save as much of the money I get so that I can pay for you to come and visit us in Youngstown. Wouldn't that be great?

I am enclosing a picture of some of my rugs and some made by other Slovaks here in Youngstown. Also I'm enclosing a picture of a loom, which is what mine will look like hopefully when Michael is finished building it.

I hope Martin and your girls and their children are relaxing now that the fall harvest is finished.
Your loving sister,
Mária

Author's archive.

Julia Dursa's Wedding

28 Nov 1931

To the right of the bride, Julia, is Justina (Esther), and to the left of Julia is her sister Vera. To the left of Vera is our sister Anna's daughter, Mary Sopkovich Layko. In the back row on the far left is our brother Eliáš' son and our nephew Miško, (skip one young man) then there is the groom John Lesnak, and to his right is Steve Layko. At the end of the row, to the far right is sister Anna's son (Dr.) Nick Sopkovich. Author's archive.

November 30, 1931. Youngstown, Ohio *Ked' sa dve srdcia, spoja v jedno.*
                                                    (When two hearts become one, that is the best.)

My dearest sister Katka,

I am sending you a picture of the wedding of my youngest child, Julia, and her dearest new husband, John Lesnak, whose parents are from Teblička, a Slovak village just west of Poráč. The wedding was November 28th held at St. Mary's Church here in Youngstown, with a dinner reception in the church hall. It was a lovely wedding, and Julia and John will live in our house, at 718, just next door.

Justina came home from Chicago in July since her job at Western Electric Company, maker of telephones, closed. Susanna (Suzi as she likes to be called) came with her, but Susanna and I had a bad falling out after two days when I discovered that she was smoking in the upstairs bathroom. So she left in a big huffy puff and took a train to Yonkers where my other daughter Sophie and her family live. And I almost had a falling out with Justina over a letter that came here from Chicago from a "George Zirbes." I opened it, (it is my house), but of course I couldn't understand anything because it was written in English. I was shocked when I saw the enclosed photo of Esther in a 1931 car on the driver's side! Now I'm pretty sure she smokes, and I guess she also drives a car? When she saw that I had opened the letter, she was very angry with me, but I was angry too because this man's name "Zirbes" didn't sound Slovak at all. That was when she snapped at me and said that George's nationality, German, was not important. It didn't matter that he wasn't Slovak. *Ježiš, Mária.* Is that what happens when you go to Chicago?

She said that she and George met at a dancehall in Chicago called "White City" where she and her sister Sue would go to meet other young people (or in plain words, to find boys!). I yelled with my Slovak temper, "That's how you find a boyfriend in Chicago?" That was when she snapped right back at me and said, "You think you know what's right for me. You need to keep out of my friendship with George, and if you don't, I'll be on a train heading back to Chicago and not even stay for Julia's wedding. All of those 'wonderful Slovak men' that you have tried to match make me with just look at my chin and say 'sorry' in their eyes. You don't even know what I have had to endure with a disfigured face because of some sister's carelessness, allowing me to fall from a very high porch onto a pile of rocks at age 2. Even in school, boys on the playground would point to my disfigured chin, laugh, and say, 'no chinny chin chin.' Mama, my life has not been easy."

Then she told me that this George Zirbes was not critical of her face because he too had to live through insults when he was called "Shorty" because he was only 5'4" tall. At this point she bowed her head and said softly that at age 26 she could not be fussy if she ever wanted to marry. Her face was red, her eyes were wet with tears, and she slowly went upstairs to the bedroom. I heard the door close.

Katka, I hope they do not become serious and marry, so I will try to be nicer to her and hope that she doesn't want to return to Chicago. I still remember that terrible day of her accident in Lemont. The doctor was not able to set her broken chin, and my poor child was in such pain. It was one of those terrible days I will never forget.

Katka, there's never a day when everything goes well. I will pray for my daughter, Justina.

Hellos to your family.
Your loving sister,
Mária

69

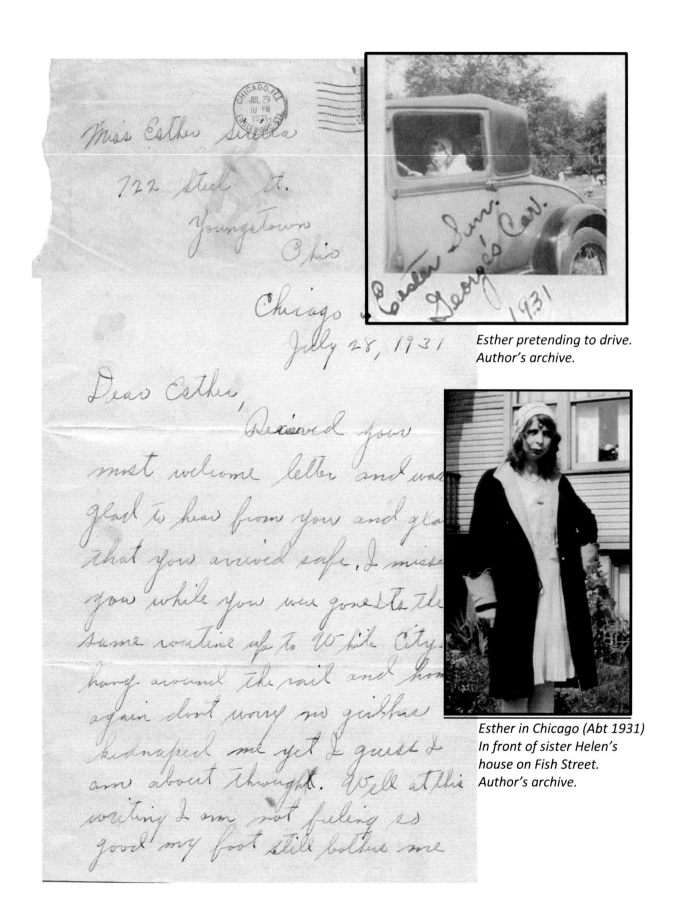

Miss Esther Sirilla

722 Steel St.

Youngstown

Ohio

Chicago

July 28, 1931

Esther pretending to drive.
Author's archive.

Dear Esther,

Received your most welcome letter and was glad to hear from you and glad that you arrived safe, I missed you while you were gone. It's the same routine up to White City. hang around the rail and home again don't worry no girl has kidnaped me yet I guess I am about thought. Well at this writing I am not feeling so good my foot still bothers me

Esther in Chicago (Abt 1931)
In front of sister Helen's
house on Fish Street.
Author's archive.

June 15, 1934 Youngstown, OH   *Ak na prvého mája večer prši, bude celý rok pekne.*
                                (If it rains on the 1st of May, the weather will be nice all year.)

My dearest sister Katka,

I always remember the saying about the rain on the first of May bringing nice weather the whole year thereafter. There are many times when I think back to our simple life in Star Junction and the closeness to nature that reminded me so much of our life in Poráč. I must tell you one of my fondest memories:

It was a warm June morning in Star Junction as I gazed out the kitchen window toward our outhouse and the surrounding ridge. Suddenly I saw a doe's head, barely visible just above the high grass. Next to her was her new fawn, still wet with afterbirth. The fawn was able to walk around, in and out of the mother's gaze, while the mother doe was trying very hard to lick and clean the new baby.

I don't know that much about deer, but I sure do know the work it takes giving birth, and I can truly understand the doe's need to rest! I watched her lay down in the soft grass, and I gazed at this scene for almost an hour.   The men were off to the mine and the children weren't awake yet.   Even after that hour of rest, the doe was still licking the new fawn and enjoying the comfort of the warm grass.

Guess who was sitting on a nearby fencepost watching this whole event? a magpie, probably thinking "My, my, the new fawn doesn't come out of an egg chirping 'hello'." A ground hog appeared for a few minutes standing high on a rock, but the scene didn't interest him as much as it did for the magpie.

The next morning, guess what? The doe came out of the woods with TWO fawns! Birthing twins is a bigger job than I know. The fawns looked quite big for newborns, with HUGE ears, almost as large as their mother's.

After the children awoke and watched the new fawn twins hobble around their mother, we all went picking mushrooms, which were very plentiful this particular summer due to so much spring rain.

Katka, this city living in Youngstown is not all so wonderful.   The air smells like iron, and the heat from the steel mills is sometimes 100 degrees F. during the summer. I just had to share with you one of my fondest memories of rural Pennsylvania because today is a day when I feel very homesick.

I hope that you too will have a special doe and new twin fawns in Rudňany!
Your loving sister,
Mária

Author's photo.

Envelope to Koterbachy (Rudňany)

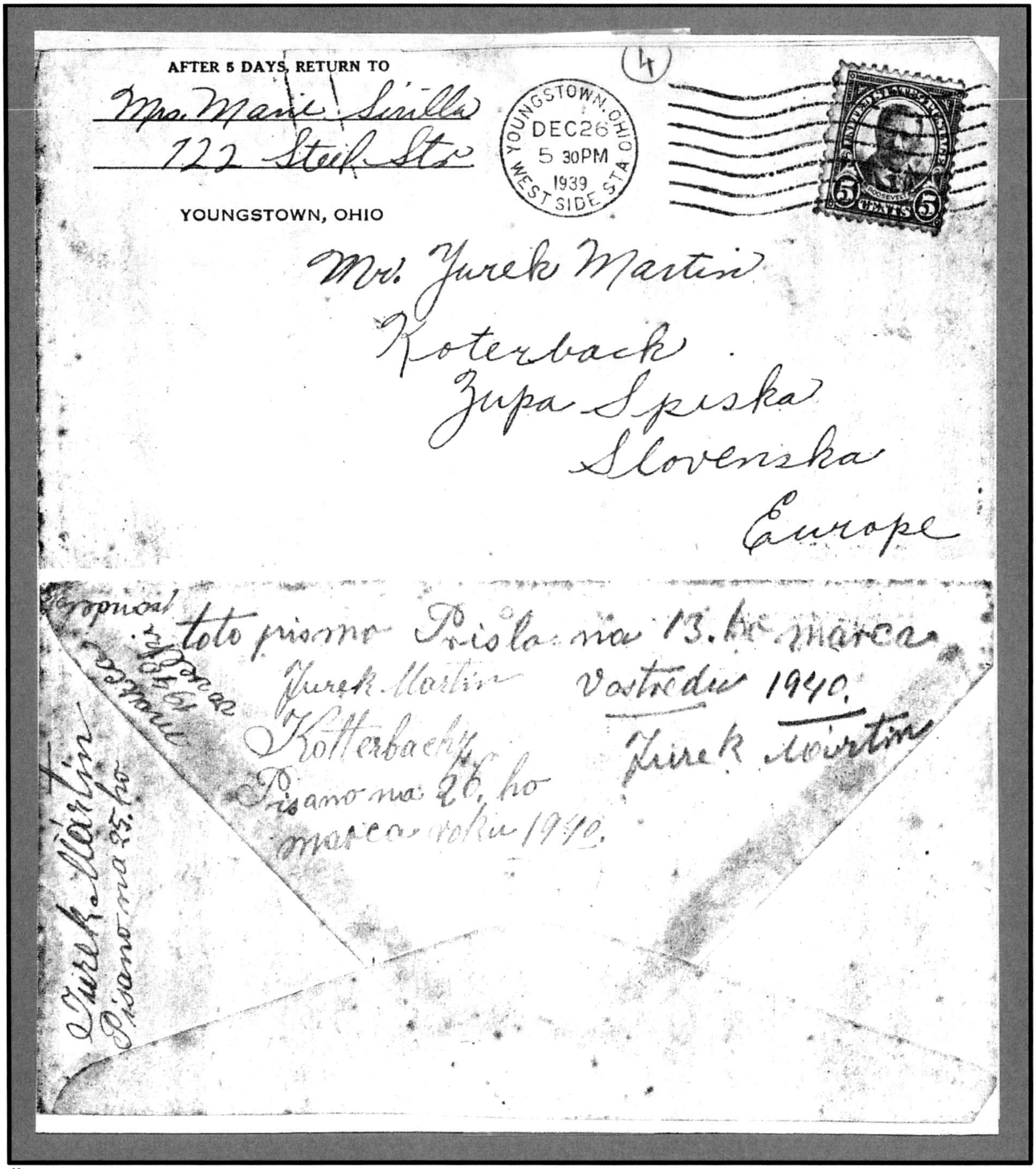

Š. Cvengroš archive.

ati mate sesünki

2

ami sesüm zisli …
me rano prisli …
dobri koje to tane …
zabrataz trojch …
Iva jane vitika …
mishova uspve …
tomi katka jan …
jim bute dobri …
anorinki lem …
čorni mia tapis …
tohochlapa kin …
hv nebute ter …
bi tamu preba …
pui sol ale to …
vas pozīrar …
nasto razi …
nastorazi i t.
i najk i Gosu …
chlopan i zd …
la čitat vaso …
ho zvatili bot …
takoho čoje …
taus vam nemam čopisati lem
douvičina apiste esei druhi vas
ti i kaña zestra vas pozīraveuje i
i nevista sitki Jovetna gutbaj
z Bohom zestro boneznam čito

**DURCA RITES WILL
BE HELD FRIDAY**

**Youngstown Man Born In
Czechoslovakia 61
Years Ago**

Funeral services for Michael Durca, who died yesterday at his home, 722 Steel, will be held at 8:30 a. m. Friday at the residence and at 9 a. m. at St. Mary's Greek Catholic church. Burial will be in St. Mary's cemetery. The body has been removed from the Vaschak funeral home to his home.

Mr. Durca was born in Czechoslovakia 61 years ago, and lived here for 10 years coming from Lemont, Pa. He was a member of St. John the Baptist Lodge 543, and Sojedenia, G. C. U.

Surviving are his widow, Mary; two daughters, Mrs. Veronica Pallo and Mrs. Julia Lesnak of Youngstown; five step-daughters, Mrs. Catherine Durca of Lemont, Mrs. Sophia Kuchta and Susan Shirilla of Yonkers, N. Y., Mrs. Helen Kostelnik and Justina Shirilla of Chicago; two step-sons, Michael and Joseph Shirilla of Yonkers; three sisters, Mrs. Mary Pacan, Mrs. Helen Durica and Mrs. Catherine Moltan, of Uniontown, Pa., and three brothers, George and Joseph of Uniontown, and Peter of Czechoslovakia.

larzu zmebuli toz
aña nevi zerabam
pisem želemčula
u Zahavsi
oter pukks biva a
ki nebuli vetro
eporzenili možeus
a asitko Iraho
jan sekije is
talem so bichrae
neskaro jak
keti planozro
evatila kebimi
sam čopisati lem
tro i lvohachlopa
arijem ketziju
abosina na stovay
i moja jeela is
Zebis mi otpisa
ul Ženati jak
enatoho lem
hurk uspetzroki
zemajte Jabri
biste nezaba
pozīraveuje i Sinami
jela is pisno
nebut ostatna

Pisani list na 9ko oktora 1935
yungston oh

Slava i Jezukhristu milo asunno · pozdravina
naj vamperse ot miloho panaboha atak ot mariji
virilla Du amojej fameliji · dto pretebe katko imar
x cina taik ss vas bars krasni pozdravujem moja
buba ser ... Želem
nebar ... vam
vinčujem ...
ta i mar ...
mojo či ...
hlopa j ...
cne bole ...
ka prim ...
sama ...
atak it ...
komen ...
ca moja ...
ti opači ...
mebuli ...
uagust ...
ko tum ...
žili ko ...
čo sem ...
hanasebars ...
tane chtila a ...
osetem hotin zmeisli Donevjorku nasa ta umetam
buli Jatvanac najvaksi so apojum naresterant
tomar vzal hanin kurder vun donej skraju prisol

Mary Dursa, (Abt 1935). Author's archive.

9 October 1935 Youngstown, OH   *Moja drahá žena.*   (My loving wife.)

My dearest sister Katka ,
Praise be to Jesus Christ. Heartfelt greetings to you Katka and your husband Martin. I am not feeling so good and am often very weak. I received your letter and thank you for the photo, although I see that you look a little fat. I hope you are not weak as I am.

I am sad to say it is almost one year since my second husband, Michael Dursa, died. He was so good and now he is gone and I am alone and lonesome to be by myself. Michael went to God. I often go to the cemetery at St. Mary's Church and look at the grave. It feels like the grave site is my home. I bought a nice tombstone with the word **žena** (wife) *for my side, and it was not cheap. It cost me $300. This will be my future home. I've put my real first name, "**Maria**" and my maiden name "**Duricza**," in addition to "**zena**," on the stone.*

My son Michael came to visit from Yonkers, but he didn't stay long, which is too bad because I wanted to buy him a palinka (brandy).

Katka, our sister Anna and I were on vacation in New York in August for two weeks, visiting my daughter Sophie, my son Mike, and my daughter Sue, who all live in Yonkers. We went to the ocean at Rockaway Beach and went swimming in the Atlantic. The sight of the ocean and its great distance brought back memories for me of my first crossing with Anna from Bremenhaven to New York. I said to Anna, "Let's go back to visit the old country and our homeland." But Anna said she did not want to go, and she is right, it is not a safe time now to go back home to the old country.

(Author's note: Mária had made 3 crossings from Bremenhaven to New York prior to 1935.)

Anna doesn't look very good. Her leg hurts and she feels weak.   With the help of the Blessed Mother of God and many prayers, I hope she will have better health. Some other news is that I heard that our brother John exchanged his farm for two houses. Some other news is that my son Joe's daughter June is studying to be a teacher at Youngstown University.

Katka, here it is very cold, and it is only October. Everything is very expensive. The news is full of the US going to war. And we have problems with the black people right here in Youngstown.

Please write how you are and take care of your husband as long as he lives. When he dies, it is too late, so do not argue with him when he does something stupid. Forgive him. I would not ever argue with my husband should he come back, but he cannot come back.

So my dear sister, I don't have anything more to write, but I send greetings to you and your family, your husband Martin and your daughter Katka.   My son Joe and his wife Cate, our sister Anna and her sons, and my daughter Julia, her husband John, and their daughter Margie all send you their greetings.

Gutbye , who knows, this letter could be my last.

Your loving sister, Mária

Oh, I forgot, let me know if the priest's son got married before he was consecrated. Here they do not consecrate married men, only single ones.

UNITED STATES OF AMERICA

DECLARATION OF INTENTION
(Invalid for all purposes seven years after the date hereof)

No. 237238

STATE OF OHIO
MAHONING COUNTY } ss:

In the ___ COMMON PLEAS ___ Cou
of MAHONING COUNTY at YOUNGSTOWN, OHIO

I, MERY DURSA
now residing at 722 STEEL STREET, YOUNGSTOWN MAHONING OHIO (State)
occupation HOUSEWIFE, aged 66 years, do declare on oath that my personal description is:
Sex FEMALE, color WHITE, complexion FAIR, color of eyes BROWN
color of hair GREY, height 5 feet 7 inches; weight 165 pounds; visible distinctive ma.
None
race SLOVAK; nationality CZECHO SLOVAK
I was born in PORACS HUNGARY NOW CZECHOSLOVAKIA on DEC. 23 1871
I am WIDOW married. The name of my wife or husband was MICHAEL DURSA
we were married on JULY 19 1910, at NEW SLEM, PENNA.; she or he wa
born at HUNGARY, on UNKNOWN, entered the United State
at UNKNOWN, on, for permanent residence therein, and no
resides DECEASED. I have 9 children, and the name, date and place of birt
and place of residence of each of said children are as follow KATHERINE DURITZA BORN 1892 at HUNGARY
resides UNIONTOWN, PA. SOFIA KUPTA BORN 1897 AT BROWNFIELD, PA. RESIDES
NEW YORK, N. Y. MICHAEL BORN 1898 AT VANDERBILT, PA. RESIDES NEW YORK, N.
JOSEPH BORN 1900 at LEMONT PA. RESIDES YO.O. HELEN KOSTELNIK BORN 1903
at LEMONT PA. RESIDES CHICAGO, ILLINOIS.
I have NOT heretofore made a declaration of intention. Number, on (Date)
at (City or town)
my last foreign residence was PORACS HUNGARY NOW CZECHO SLOVAKIA
I emigrated to the United States of America from BREMEN GERMANY (Country)
my lawful entry for permanent residence in the United States was at NEW YORK, N.Y. (State)
under the name of MARIA SIRILA, on FEB. 6 1896
on the vessel S S SPREE
(If other than by vessel, state manner of arrival)
I will, before being admitted to citizenship, renounce forever all allegiance and fidelity to any foreign prince, potentat
state, or sovereignty, and particularly, by name, to the prince, potentate, state, or sovereignty of which I may be at the tin
of admission a citizen or subject; I am not an anarchist; I am not a polygamist nor a believer in the practice of polygamy; a
it is my intention in good faith to become a citizen of the United States of America and to reside permanently therein; and
certify that the photograph affixed to the duplicate and triplicate hereof is a likeness of me: SO HELP ME GOD.

mery Dursa

Subscribed and sworn to before me in the office of the Clerk of said Co
at YOUNGSTOWN, OHIO this 7th day of OCTOBER
anno Domini 19 38 Certification No. xxxxxxx from the Commis-
sioner of Immigration and Naturalization showing the lawful entry of
declarant for permanent residence on the date stated above, has been recei
by me. The photograph affixed to the duplicate and triplicate hereof is a like
ness of the declarant.

7X16913
[SEAL]

WILLIAM F. QUINLAN
Clerk of the COMMON PLEAS C
By Helen H. Smith Deputy Cle.

Form 2202-L-A
U. S. DEPARTMENT OF LABOR
IMMIGRATION AND NATURALIZATION SERVICE

14—2623
U. S. GOVERNMENT PRINTING OFFICE

mery Dursa

(left margin, vertical text)
No. 26745 JUSTINA ZURA BORN 1905 at LEMONT, PA. RESIDES CHICAGO, ILLINOIS. JULIA LESNAK BORN
SUSANNA BORN 1907 at LEMONT, PA. RESIDES YONKERS N.Y.
VERA DURSA PALLO BORN 1911 at LEMONT, PA. RESIDES YO.O.
1913 at VANDERBILT PA. RESIDED YOUNGSTOWN O.
(Zurbes)

Author's note: Mária's height is listed as 5'7", with brown eyes and weight of 165 lbs. She was 67 years.

June 24, 1941 Youngstown, OH *Ja som pyšná, že som Američanka.* (I am proud to be an American.)

My dearest sister Katka,

Today should be a day of celebration, but I am both thankful and saddened by my receiving my American citizenship today. It has been 44 years that I have lived in Ameryka, and now after all of this time, I am finally an American citizen. The new Alien Registration Act, or Smith Act, was signed into law on June 28, 1940 and required aliens to register at their local post office, requiring them to give details of race, address, relatives in the US, organization memberships, application for citizenship and of course requiring fingerprinting. Since neither my first nor second husbands were naturalized, <u>I was considered an alien</u> all of these years and had to go through this registration process, even though I had applied to be a naturalized citizen on October 7, 1938. The government said that this alien registration was a patriotic duty, whatever that means. We were told that the foreign population of the US should not be alarmed about this alien registration process. Well, who could not worry about the chance of the police coming to your door and your property being taken away?

Anna Matej, my neighbor and friend who was one of my sponsors at the naturalization hearing at the Mahoning County Courthouse today, left me at my house this afternoon. No one was home yet. (Vera's children were in school, Dutch her husband was working at the steel mill, and Vera was working at her housecleaning job.) So I headed right down the stairs to my wine cellar! My cabarnet grapes make the best wine, so I poured myself a glass of last year's wine and stared out to the garden and grape vines in disbelief that I really passed the naturalization test, despite my *broken English.* I am grateful to our priest at St. Mary's Church who organized a citizenship class in Slovak to help prepare us for the naturalization test's questions. Today, though, I was given some pretty easy questions like: Who is the President of the United States? What is the name of the capital of the United States? Is the United States founded on religious freedom? I had no problem answering those easy questions!
I was lucky about a new rule too that stated:

    Certain applicants, because of age and time as a permanent resident, are exempt from the English requirements for naturalization and may take the test in their native language.

Since I am 69 years old and have lived in the US for 44 years, I qualified for this exemption. So my friend Anna Matej translated the questions for me into Slovak! Thus I was able to pass.

Katka, this doesn't mean that I have forgotten you and Slovakia, despite the trouble now in 1941 of Monsignor Josef Tiso, who had to accept Adolf Hitler's demand for Slovakia's independence from Czechoslovakia. I am just thankful that I own my house here and have our sister Anna close by. Now that I am a US citizen, no one can take this property away from me. I have to tell you how lucky Anna is because her husband, Joseph, became a naturalized citizen on March 19, 1900, and at that time she, his wife, automatically became a US citizen without doing anything! Lucky for Anna.

I hope you understand what I am saying: I am still a Slovak- speaking woman with my love forever for the country of my birth. My new US citizenship is a necessity, but it doesn't change what's in my heart.

Katka, write to me about the new politics in Slovakia and give my hellos to your family.
Your loving sister,
Mária

Pledge of Allegiance

Students giving the pledge of allegiance to the flag using the "Bellamy salute" (Hail Caesar), which was changed to "hand on heart" in June, 1942. Courtesy of Wikimedia Commons, public domain.

I pledge
Allegiance to the Flag
of the
United States of America,
and to the Republic
for which it stands
one Nation (under God), (added in 1954)
indivisible,
with Liberty and Justice for All.

July 1, 1941 Youngstown, OH   *Zahryznút' si do jazyka.* (Bite your tongue.)

My dearest sister Katka,

I often think back to our life in Star Junction, Pennsylvania when the children were all about and many times too lively. I especially remember an evening, about the end of May in 1915, almost the end of the school year, when I nearly lost my mind. All of the young Sirilla girls, Sue, Justina, Helen, and Anna still attended school at our two- room Patch Schoolhouse; the Dursa girls, Vera and Julia, were still too young for school. My two boys were working in the mine; Sophie was working as a maid, but she also helped me out at home. Here is my memory:

The winter had finally melted away into a beautiful spring and now even a summer seemed possible. The goslings were huddled around their mothers, enjoying the taste of new grass, and our potatoes and cabbage plants in the garden had sprung into visible growth while Michael and I sat on the porch for a few minutes of rest from our long workday. He still had some black coal streaks on his forehead, and I still had some pieces of raw dough on my fingernails from my bread baking, but the smells of the earth and the companionship of my husband, alone, for a few minutes were refreshing.

This "quiet time" came quickly to an end when we heard a chorus of sounds coming from all of the girls: five girls all together saying something over and over and Sophie telling them that they must practice until they were perfect. So I ran into the house and saw all four schoolgirls and their "home teacher," Sophie, at the kitchen table with their books in front of them reciting the "**Pledge of allegiance to the flag of the United States of America.**" And as I stood by the front door observing this scene, they, not knowing I was watching, proceeded to recite the pledge one more time with Sophie.

That was when I lost my mind. I stormed into the kitchen, threw all of the books from the table on to the floor, and yelled at the top of my voice,
   Nenos tvoje americké knihy do môjho domu! (**Do not bring your American books into my house!**)
Sophie tried to explain for the younger girls that the teacher insisted that every student be able to recite the "Pledge of Allegiance to the Flag" by heart on the last day of school. And that the girls did not all know it perfectly yet and had to practice. But that did not help soothe my anger because every American book and every American flag and every American activity from school only took my children farther and farther away from my influence as their mother.

And so Katka, I never saw another school book in the house again. Sophie later told me that the girls would hide their schoolbooks under a big rock in the neighbor's yard.

Now 26 years later, and having had to recite that very "Pledge of Allegiance to the Flag" at **my** swearing-in-ceremony at the Mahoning County Courthouse on June 24, 1941 for the official granting of my naturalized US citizenship, I feel so sorry to have been so mean to *moje krásne dievčatá,* (my beautiful girls). It is too late to say I am sorry now. They will only remember that I made them keep all of their American schoolbooks out of the house. *Bože môj, Bože môj.* (Oh my God, my God.)

Katka, I know that 6 of your 8 children died of diseases at an early age and that the emptiness in your heart can never be filled. I am very thankful to have lost only 1 baby out of 12. I just wish that when I was younger, I would not have had so much of that "**Slovak temper.**" But it is never too late for me to practice to control what I say! I am thinking of you.
Your loving sister, Mária

Gravesite of Martin Jurek

Burial October, 1941, Poráč for Martin Jurek, Cemetery of St. Demetrius Church. Later two grandsons were added: Michal Cvengroš (1992) and Štefan Cvengroš (2002). Author's photo.

October 30, 1941 Youngstown, OH   *Niekedy život je ako krásna rozprávka.*
                                    (Sometimes life is like a beautiful fairy tale.)

My dearest sister Katka,

I am writing for all of your family here in Ohio and Pennsylvania, sending you our deepest sympathy upon hearing that your beloved husband, Martin, died on October 3rd. We must always be prepared for sadness and loved ones dying, but when the actual death occurs, we are too often spiritually empty. I can still remember way back in the 1890s when all of us siblings could only think of one thing: emigrating to Ameryka. But Martin took you aside and promised if you stayed in Poráč, he would marry you and build you a house on his inherited property in Koterbachy (Rudňany). And that is what happened, and together you built a good life, despite many hardships. We are all thinking of you.

On the bright side I want to tell you about a book that I found at our church last Sunday as Anna and I were leaving. It is called *Povesť o Slovákoch* (The Legend about the Slovaks.) Here is a brief summary of the part that I liked the most:

The Lord met with the many nations living in the old country who had become so numerous that they had to disperse to other parts of the world. The Slovaks came at the very end of the group of nations to meet the Lord. The Lord said, "Well, you are such a little nation, what shall I give you? The greater nations have already received the lands, power, and glory." The Slovaks said, "We are not asking for great lands or power or glory; we are asking for only one thing: your love, dear Lord." The Lord said, "You shall have my love; I shall love the Slovak nation forever." But the Lord felt that the Slovaks needed more than just his love, so he put his finger onto the Slovaks' tongues and said, "I am giving you the most beautiful language in the whole world. The Slovak language will sound like the singing of the angels. It will be as pleasant as a breeze in May and its sounds will make the hearts of young and old alike grow younger."

Then he found the most beautiful songs and put them into the Slovak mouths and said, "I am giving you also the most beautiful songs so that when your women start to sing, the birds will fall silent, the brooks will start sparkling and the hills will jump a little. The singing will turn your country into a paradise."
And because all good things come in threes, the Lord said, "I am giving you also a beautiful land under the Tatra mountains for your home. Even if you have to suffer to keep this land, do not give up for I shall remember you with a Father's heart and always help you."

And so the Slovaks have lived under the Tatra Mountains for more than a thousand years serving the Lord who protects them and singing about anything in beautiful melodic sounds of the Slovak language. Sometimes life is like a beautiful fairy tale!

Katka, there was also another story in this book about Juraj Janošík, the famous Slovak hero who stole from the rich and gave to the poor. You remember our father often telling his best Janošík story about the huge fires that Janošík and his followers set *na Kráľova holʼa* (on the top of King's Mountain) which could be seen from Poráč. He said the fires were so huge that they could even be seen from Budapest! Then all of us would laugh and imagine Janošík sternly warning the Hungarians in Budapest to "beware of us Slovaks who are looking down at you from up here high in the Tatra Mountains."

Katka, I hope these stories will cheer you up a little bit and help you forget your sadness. All of us in Youngstown and Pennsylvania are sending you and your family our deepest sympathy.
Your loving sister,
Mária

World War II Navy recruits

Sailor boys: Michael Kuchta; Friend, name unknown; Joseph Kuchta. Author's archive.

Michael (Miško) Dyuritza at the Navy barracks in Hawaii. M. Peel archive.

April 5, 1945 Youngstown, OH   *Kristus Voskres!* (Christ is Risen!) *Haleluja.*

My dearest sister Katka,

On Easter Sunday we attended mass and had our Easter food baskets blessed at St. Mary's Church. Our basket contained: *šunka* (ham); *hrudka* (egg cheese); *chren* (beets and horseradish); *klobása* (sausage); *páska* (sweet bread) ; *pysanky* (decorated eggs); *mákovník & orechovník* (poppy seed & walnut rolled coffee cakes); a special Easter decorated candle; and a hand embroidered cross stitch coverlet over the basket made by our sister Anna.

We all hope by next Easter that the war will be over. Here we have endured more than 3 ½ years of food rationing and the enlistments of my grandsons, most of them sent to the Pacific area.

All of Sophie's boys are now serving in the military as is my adopted nephew Miško. Sophie says that her family has all branches of the military represented: **Navy**: Joe Kuchta and Michael Kuchta; **Army**: Andrew Kuchta; **Coast Guard**: son-in-law Collin Blick; **Air Force**: son-in-law John Cleary. My nephew Miško is also serving in the **Navy**.

On this Easter Sunday, April 1, a huge fleet of ships assembled in the Pacific and began the invasion of Okinawa. I hope "my sailor boys" are not in this battle. Miško enlisted in the Navy in 1939 from Detroit, Michigan. He said he was going to visit his sister Esther in Michigan. Well, right after he enlisted, he was assigned to the ship *USS Quincy*, which was **sunk** during a battle near Quadalcanal. Then Miško was assigned to the *USS Wharton* and finally to the *USS Santa Fe*, which was stationed in Pearl Harbor. Katka, I am so thankful that my Miško was not injured or killed when the *USS Quincy* sunk! We get all of this information about the war from our Slovak radio station in Pittsburgh.

I'm sure you heard the news of the Normandy Invasion of June 6, 1944, when American and British troops crossed the English Channel and landed on the shores of Normandy joining French army troops. After liberating Paris, these troops crossed the Rhine River, moving toward Berlin, Germany, hoping to end this horrible war soon, with the Soviet troops joining from the east.

We have also heard about the battle at Dukla Pass on the eastern border of Slovakia and Ukraine, with Ukrainian and Slovak soldiers battling and dying at the hands of the Germans. We hear that so many Slovak villages east of Poráč were burned down by the retreating Germans, leaving Slovaks homeless and many dead, buried in mass graves. This is why the war must end. However, I worry about the Soviet Union becoming the new Slovak boss.

We also heard about the failure of the Slovak National Uprising (*Slovenské národné povstanie* or SNP) (which began on August 29, 1944), to overthrow the German occupiers. We heard that the Slovak partisans and the Soviets were overcome by the Germans, and according to our Slovak radio station, by March, 1945, just a month ago, the Germans had murdered almost 4,000 Slovaks and put almost 15,000 Slovaks in concentration camps as a punishment for the attempted overthrow. I'm sure when the Germans lose the war, President Tiso will be killed and "Independent Slovakia" will disappear, along with Adolf Hitler.

I only understand some of these politics. I just hope that the war ends soon and that Sophie's boys and my Miško will all come home alive. I am sure that these years of German occupation have given you and others in Spiš severe hardships, too. I have read many times your letter telling how important your vegetable garden and fruit orchard in Rudňany are for your survival and how tough is the rationing of sugar, flour, butter, shoes, etc. I know how thrifty you are because I saw with my own eyes in 1909 when your daughter María outgrew her woolen sweater, you unraveled the yarn and knitted it into socks!

You will probably not receive this letter because the Germans are running **out** of your country and the Soviets are running **in**, and the post office is probably closed for good. However, if you are lucky to receive this letter, I only hope that you will not get in trouble for this anti-war talk.

We all think of you and your family during these sad times, and we know that spring is rebirth and renewal in the fields and in our hearts. *Haleluja, chvál'me Boha* (Alleluja, praise God).
Happy Easter.

Your loving sister,
 María

Slovenská stará mamička, pekných vel'kych synov máte, ale ich na vojnu date. Ach..vojna..vojna..vojna.
(Slovak grandmother, you have beautiful grandsons, but they must go to war. Oh, war, war, war.)

Blessing Easter baskets in the village of Torysky, Slovakia.
From Spiš, a Pearl of Slovakia, by Ladislav Jiroušek, 2000, p. 56.

September 30, 1945   Youngstown, OH   *D'akujeme vám za vaš list.* (Thank you for your letter.)

My dearest sister Katka,

Heartfelt greetings to you and all of the Jurek and Cvengroš family at #261 Rudňany. Yes, the terrible war is over and now we have to give thanks that all of Sophie's boys and my dear nephew Miško are all alive and will return home soon. Your last letter arrived with much heartbreak to hear of the very serious hardships suffered in Slovakia, especially as the Germans were retreating and the Soviets were chasing them out. When you said that the *Potraviny* (grocery store) in Rudňany was closed, I know now that you are much more deprived than we here in Youngstown, so I am preparing a package for you with some of the items you requested, and I hope this meets with smiles from all of your family.

I can't send real oranges so I am sending Vitamin C tablets. I am including packages of dried chocolate pudding;   several bars of Hersey's chocolate candy; a large can of Folger's instant coffee; several packages of black tea; several packets of sugar cubes; and several packets of dried egg powder. Last are several packages of cigarettes that you can give to your son-in-law Štefan. For your sewing, I am including heavy dark blue material to make pants for the older boys along with white cotton for making them new shirts. For Margita, your youngest grandchild, who now is 12 years old, I am including a pair of shoes, based on the size of the drawing of her foot that you sent and some flowery cotton material that you can use for sewing her a new dress or blouse. Last I am including several skeins of yarn for knitting, either socks or sweaters which would be needed by someone, I'm sure.

When I think of how the Germans tried to steal as much as possible in their retreat west, and then the Soviets came in pursuit and took what was left, I know it will take years to "forget" this kind of pilfering and carnage that war brings. I hope that you will receive our package. I am sending it c/o St. Demetrius Church in Poráč because several other members of our church here in Youngstown are also sending packages to family through your church which hopefully is a safer receiver than your home address.

Katka, last night I awoke from a dream that I was back in Poráč. As I awoke I could still see the whole dream again, seeing Spišský hrad, our favorite castle, to the east and the High Tatra Mountains to the northwest. You and I were young, walking home from the sheep barn, carrying our fresh brynza cheese and singing our favorite song, one that we all learned in school: *Daj Boch šťastia celej zemi.* (Lord, kindly bless all of this our country.)   My favorite line is the last line of the third verse, *D opraj Bože svojmu dielu večné trvanie.* (May the world last forever, O my Lord, we pray.) We were so young and so happy.

Katka, this war is finally over, and we all give you our greetings knowing that your life will improve with time and sunshine. We hope you receive our package and enjoy what's inside.
Your loving sister,
Mária

From Slovak Heritage Live, January, 1993, p.9.

Pottery from Pozdišovce

Tanier s tancujúcimi dievčatami (Plate with dancing girls). By Andrej Cizmárik, Pozdišovce, Slovakia. Author's photo.

June 1, 1946 Youngstown, OH *Kde je Slovák, tam je pieseň!*

                        (Where there is a Slovak, there is a song.)

My dearest sister Katka,

I am sending you hugs and wishes for improvement in your health. I, too, have had days when I have pain in my legs and back and can barely walk and need help getting up the stairs to my bed. Sometimes I sleep here in the living room on the sofa where it is cool and quiet.

Yesterday when I was feeling better, I walked down Steel Street to the home of my friend, Anna Matej. She was one of my witnesses for my American citizenship. Upon entering Anna's kitchen, my eyes immediately were directed to a beautiful Slovak plate hanging on the wall from the village of Pozdišovce, the ever popular *tanier s tancujucimi dievčatami (*plate with dancing girls). I remember seeing the same plate in your kitchen in Rudňany during my visit in 1909. I also remember when we were young our singing the song *"A harčare dobri chlopi"* about Slovakia's oldest pottery, producing many plates and vases with the dancing girls' design since the year 1500.   So how did Anna, my friend in Youngstown, get this lovely plate made in Pozdišovce?

Here is what she told me:

My nephew was an Air Force pilot during World War II. He and many other American pilots were stationed at the American Air Force base in Bari, Italy and flew B-17 bombers from Italy to locations in Germany.   Most of the bombing missions' route was over Slovakia. During one of these missions, he encountered trouble: 2 engines were knocked out by Germans patrolling eastern Slovakia. He thought he could head back to Italy with one engine, but as soon as he started making a reverse turn, the 3rd engine faded, and he knew that the only way to save his own life was to parachute from the plane. As his white umbrella parachute was slowly descending to the ground, he could see the black smoke of his ruined B-17.   He landed near a small village, and what do you suppose the name of that village was? Yes, it was Pozdišovce. He was helped in his rescue by a family living not far from where his parachute landed, and that family took care of him until he was able to get to Banska Bystrica and get rescued on an American cargo plane coming into Slovakia from Bari Air Force Base with food and ammunitions for the Slovak partisans and Soviets headquartered in Banska Bystrica. These groups were planning an uprising against the Germans and the Slovaks who were sympathetic to the German controlled government. The mother of the family took her "dancing girls" plate off the kitchen wall and insisted that my nephew take it home to America when the war was over as a remembrance of his stay with them in eastern Slovakia. After the war, and back in Youngstown, my nephew's mother was already deceased, so my nephew felt a good home for this treasure from Slovakia was with me, his Aunt Anna. And that is how this beautiful piece of Slovak ceramics came to Youngstown!

Katka, I hope this letter finds you healthier and that Slovakia, now returned to "Czechoslovakia," will gradually recuperate from the horrible devastation experienced at the hands of the occupying Germans. We all hope that this second "Czechoslovakia" will enable Slovakia to return to normal, since continuing as an independent Slovakia was not politically possible.   Let's hope that the once again Czechoslovakia will not be taken over by the communists, the Soviets, in the heart of Central Europe.

Zbohom, (Go with God)
Your loving sister,
Mária

Stara Matka (Grandma)

Mary Dursa, Youngstown, OH (Abt 1950 at 722 Steel Street.) Author's archive.

January 24, 1947. Youngstown, OH   *Bez práce, nie sú koláče.*
                                    (Without work, there are no cakes; or no pains, no gains.)

My dearest sister Katka,

I am sending my greetings upon hearing of your poor health. I too do not always feel good, but we must be strong. I hope you are feeling better when you read this letter.

I have to tell you a silly story that happened yesterday. My granddaughter, Margie, Julia's daughter, came bursting into my kitchen saying, "Grandma, my mother wants to borrow a kolachki pan."
I answered very harshly, *Margita, hovoriš po slovensky, prosím.* (Margie, please speak Slovak.)

Katka, I did understand her question in English, but I became so upset to hear a made up English word like *kolachki* instead of what we Slovaks call our nut roll cake, *orechovník*, or poppy seed roll cake, *makovník*.

I tried to explain to Margie how the word *kolachki* started in America, but I'm not sure she was convinced that I knew so much!! But anyway, this is what I told her:

The Slovak word for cake is *koláč* (kolach), and the word for cakes is *koláče* (kolacheh). I think the word *kolachk*i came from a couple of sources: maybe from the Czechs who pride themselves on the donut-like fruit filled cake called *koláč* with a smaller version of this donut cake called *koláčky* or even smaller one called *koláčik*. The word *kolachki* could also have come from the Croatian word for cakes, *kolači* (kolachee), which are powder-sugar-coated dough balls fried in oil.

Before I gave her the pan she requested, I just couldn't stop, and I had to say a few more words about the word used in America for head scarf, *babushka*.

 I told Margie that the scarf on my head is called in Slovak *šatka* (shatka) and not *babushka*!! A *babuška* is the word in Russian for an older woman or a grandma.

Well, I'm not sure Margie was listening to all of this, but at least I tried to give her the correct meanings for words that here in the English language are incorrect! *Bože môj , Bože* môj. (My God, My God).

Katka, I hope you are feeling better.
I am thinking of you.
Your loving sister,
 Mária

Slovak orechovník: walnut rolled cake. Author's photo.

1

Pisani list na 12 ho Marca 1947

Slava i Isusu Kristu milo akrasno pozdravina naj...
Sam perse ot v. viloho panaboha atak ot tvojej sestri mark...
Dursa toje potebe Sestro katko Jurek taje sestro katko
bars krasni pozdravujem naslo razi tati pisem želem dostala
trajopismo na Teba ...

Mary Dursa, Youngstown, OH (Abt 1945). Author's archive.

...roki dokraju asi kopot visiju ... atipisem želu često zberaju dokraj...
nachudobnich u cerkvi zberaju tami otpis či inaporač daco daju
janemislim a i Helena Dursa mipisala žesipuj pisala amame itu
esi gimu isnih nemas ani vanka viti čolakazima

12 March 1947   Ja nemám teraz duševný pokoj. (Now I do not have peace of mind.)

My dearest sister Katka Jurek:
Praise be to Jesus Christ and dear God.   Heartfelt greetings from your sister Mary Dursa.
I have received your letter dated 27th of February, but you did not have a good address on your envelope because it did not say North America, only Youngstown, Ohio. I hope when you receive this letter that your health is better.

*You know that I too was very sick for four weeks. I was very weak and couldn't work or do anything, only to fix a little something to eat. I raised my children (all 11 of them), and now nobody can hand me a cup of water! They only wait until I die and leave this world. **Yes, that is true!** When I was so sick I did think that I was going to die, but now I feel better, although I still have a terrible cough.*

Our sister Anna has sold her house here in Youngstown for $13,000 and will go to live with her son, Nick, the dentist.   Yesterday he left for business in Pittsburgh, so I went over to his house to keep Anna company and stayed overnight. It was not such a good rest because Anna didn't leave me enough blankets and the room was very cold!! I shouldn't be complaining so much.   I wish Anna had not moved away from our Steel Street neighborhood.   Campbell is like from your house in Rudňany all the way to Markušovce. So now I don't have anyone close by from Poráč, only Roman Catholics!

Now I must also tell you that everything here is very expensive, not just food but even white cloth for shirts, which is not always even available to buy. Butter costs $1.00 a pound, and meat and bacon is over $1.00 a pound. Not only is everything expensive, but we often have to stand in line to buy something! All of this is due to the horrible war, and they say that this situation might last another two years. Our church, St. Mary's Church, asks for money and/or clothing to send to the Old Country. Please let me know if anyone in Poráč received anything. As you know Youngstown has so many people with family still living in Poráč. Our sister Helena Dursa from Uniontown wrote me that in addition to your food hardships, you have had a very cold winter with snow and wind so strong that you couldn't even go outside for days.   I shouldn't complain so much!!!!

Our brother Mike, who also lives in Campbell, and his family are sending you their greetings. His son is still in a military hospital, and no one knows if his health will get better so that he can get out. My son Joe and his wife Cate are sending you greetings, and they hope that your health improves. Their 18 - year-old daughter June is studying to be a teacher at Youngstown University, and her brother Richard is a good student in the high school.   He wants to study dentistry at Ohio State University.   Joe and Cate have only these two children. My two daughters Veronica and Julia and their families are also sending you their greetings.

Katka, please write to me and tell me how you are feeling and especially what is new in Slovakia now that you are once again "Czechoslovakia."   In your previous letter you wrote that Russia is asking for Slovaks to go there and work, especially people who are doctors and nurses. You wrote that 3 women from Spiš have left already, although Russia is encouraging more men to go than women. I think it is a risky business, and I don't really trust Russian men, especially after all the horrible things we heard about them when the Russian soldiers liberated Slovakia from Hitler.   I shouldn't complain so much!!

*My dear sister, "Gutbaj" and have a Happy Easter. (**Štastnú Veľkú Noč**) I am sending kisses to all (XXX) from your sister Mary Dursa, 722 Steet St., Youngstown, Ohio, North America.*

Family Group Sheet for Katarina Durica

Husband:		Martin Jurek
	Birth:	13 Nov 1874 in Porac, Spis, Slovakia
	Death:	03 Oct 1941 in Rudnany, (Spis) Slovakia. Bur. St. Demeter's Greek Catholic Cemetery, Porac, Slovakia
	Marriage:	27 May 1896 in Porac, (Spis) Slovakia
	Father:	Jacob Jurek
	Mother:	Anna Maczaszko

Wife:		Katarina Durica
	Birth:	15 Sep 1876 in Porac, Slovakia
	Death:	19 Mar 1947 in Rudnany, Slovakia. Bur. St. Demeter's Greek Catholic Cemetery, Porac
	Father:	Michal Durica
	Mother:	Maria Mrozko

Children:

1 M	Name:	Joannes (Jan) Jurek
	Birth:	14 Feb 1897 in Porac, (Spis) Slovakia
	Death:	26 Jul 1909 in Rudnany, (Spis) Slovakia

2 F	Name:	Maria Jurek
	Birth:	09 Dec 1898 in Porac, (Spis) Slovakia
	Death:	12 Apr 1933 in Rudnany, (Spis) Slovakia
	Spouse:	Stefan Cvengros

3 F	Name:	Katarina Jurek
	Birth:	14 Apr 1900 in Porac, (Spis) Slovakia
	Death:	Aft. 1927
	Spouse:	Demeter Midlik

4 M	Name:	Martin Jurek
	Birth:	04 Oct 1901 in Porac, (Spis) Slovakia
	Death:	15 Oct 1901 in Rudnany, (Spis) Slovakia

5 M	Name:	Joannes (Jan) Jurek
	Birth:	04 Sep 1904 in Porac, Spis Slovakia
	Death:	04 Mar 1910 in Rudnany, (Spis) Slovakia

6 M	Name:	Michal Jurek
	Birth:	20 Sep 1907 in Porac, (Spis) Slovakia
	Death:	06 Dec 1910 in Rudnany, (Spis) Slovakia

7 M	Name:	Antonius Jurek
	Birth:	16 Jun 1912 in Porac, (Spis) Slovakia
	Death:	17 Nov 1915 in Rudnany, (Spis) Slovakia

April 1, 1947 Youngstown, OH   *Spomieký na našu sestru Katarínu.*
(Remembrances of our sister Katarína)
My dearest niece Katarína, at #261 Rudňany, Czechoslovakia
I, my sisters Anna and Helen, and my brothers John and Mike, are all sending you our deepest sympathy at the death of your mother and our beloved sister Katarína who died this past March 19th. She was our dearest sister, Katka, and we all loved her dearly. We extend our sadness to all of your children and the children of your deceased sister Mária.

Please write to us and tell us how you are all doing. We are so saddened to be so far away and miss attending the funeral mass in Poráč with the burial also in the Poráč cemetery, but we have asked our priest at St. Mary's Church here in Youngstown to say a mass in Katka's memory, which will be next Sunday. Sister Helen and her family will travel here from Uniontown, Pennsylvania. We will also have our sister Anna and her family, our brother Mike and his familiy, and our brother John and his family who all live here in Youngstown. Please accept our deepest sympathy from all of your family here in Ohio and Pennsylvania.

"O Pane Ježiši, udel' milost' duši odobratej na večnost', Katarína."
(O gentlest heart of Jesus, have mercy on the soul of Thy departed servant, Katarína.)

Your Aunt, *(Tetka)* Mary Dursa
Here is our prayer for our sister, Katka:

#261 Rudňany, Katka's home.

> *"The Lord bless you, and keep you;*
> *The Lord make His face shine upon you,*
> *And be gracious to you;*
> *The Lord lift up His countenance upon you,*
> *And give you peace."*
> (Numbers 6:24-26)

Kostolík Svätý Demetrius
(Chapel of St. Demeter, Poráč)

Odpočívaj v pokoji. Amen.
(Rest in Peace, Amen.) Author's photos.

93

Family Group Sheet for Anna Durica

Husband:	Joseph Sopkovich

Birth:	31 Dec 1860 in Koterbach(now Rudnany),Spis,Slovakia
Death:	11 Jul 1922 in Youngstown, OH, Bur.St Mary's Byzantine Catholic Cemetery
Marriage:	01 Jul 1892 in Latrobe, PA Naturalization:
Father:	Josef Sopkovic March 19, 1900, Fayette County, PA
Mother:	Katharina Burej

Wife:	Anna Durica

Birth:	19 Dec 1873 in Porac, Spis, Slovakia
Death:	25 Jan 1950 in Youngstown, OH Bur. St. Mary's Byzantine Cemetery
Father:	Michal Durica
Mother:	Maria Mrozko

Children:

1 F

Name:	Mary Sopkovich
Birth:	07 Jan 1893 in Brownfield, Fayette, Pennsylvania, USA
Death:	24 Mar 1935 in Youngstown, Mahoning, OH
Marriage:	09 Jun 1908 in Youngstown, Mahoning, OH
Spouse:	Stephen Layko

2 M

Name:	Stephen Sopkovich
Birth:	28 Dec 1895 in Brownfield, Fayette, Pennsylvania, USA
Death:	01 Jul 1965 in Youngstown, Mahoning, OH
Burial:	St Mary's Byzantine Catholic Church Cemetery,Youngstown,Ohio
Marriage:	24 Jul 1917 in Youngstown, Mahoning, OH; bur. cemetery of St. Mary's Byzantine Cath. Church
Spouse:	Catherine Drapp

3 M

Name:	Michael Sopkovich
Birth:	06 Sep 1899 in Brownfield, Fayette, Pennsylvania, USA
Death:	17 Jul 1990 in Youngstown, Mahoning, OH
Marriage:	02 Aug 1927 in Youngstown, Mahoning, OH
Spouse:	Anna Stanislaw

4 M

Name:	Nicholas Joseph Sopkovich
Birth:	01 Jun 1909 in Youngstown, Mahoning, OH
Death:	08 Jun 1990 in Canfield, Mahoning, Ohio, United States; Age: 81
Marriage:	18 Jul 1936 in Youngstown, Mahoning, OH
Spouse:	Catherine Brincko

SOPKOVICH—Mrs. Anna, aged 76, of Mellinger Road, R. D. 2, Canfield died 5 a. m. Wednesday in South Side Hospital. Born Dec. 19, 1873, at Porac Spiska Zupa, Slovakia, a daughter of Michael and Mary Mrozko Duritza. Her husband, Joseph Sopkovich, died in 1922. She was a founding member of St. Mary's Greek Catholic Church and a member of the National Slovak Society No. 314, Sojedenija No. 489 and the Rosary Society of St. Mary's. She leaves three sons, Stephen, Michael and Dr. Nicholas, all of Youngstown; two brothers, John Duritza of Youngstown; and Michael Dorris of Campbell; two sisters, Mrs. Mary Dursa of Youngstown and Mrs. Helen Dursa of Uniontown, Pa.; 13 grandchildren, and 17 great-grandchildren. Prayer service will be held at the Vaschak Funeral Home at 7:30 p. m. Friday. Funeral services will be held at 8:30 a. m. Saturday at the funeral home and at 9 a. m. in the church. Rev. Joseph Jackanien officiating. Interment St. Mary's Greek Catholic Cemetery. Friends may call at the funeral home Thursday and Friday from 2 to 4 and 7 to 9 p. m.
VASCHAK FUNERAL HOME   40235

Ann Sopkovich
January 25, 1950
Aged 76

Najsladšie Srdce Ježišove, vždy prítomné v Prevelebnej Sviatosti Oltárnej, vždy horiace láskou ku úbohým dušiam v Očistci, udel milosť duši odobravšej sa na večnosť. O, Pane Ježišu, nebuď prísny vo svojom rozsudku, lež daj niekoľko kvapiek Tvojej predrahej krve spadnúť na páľčivé plamene a Ty najvýš milosrdný Spasiteľu, doposli svojich anjelov, aby odprevadili dušu na večnosť sa odobravšiu na miesto pokoja, občerstvenia a svetla. Ameň.

January 26, 1950 Youngstown, OH   *Čas lieči všetky raný.* (Time heals all wounds.)

My dearest sister Helen,
I am in shock and very saddened by the death of our sister Anna yesterday. She was my best friend here in Youngstown. The funeral mass and burial will be at St. Mary's Church here in Youngstown. I hope you will be able to travel from Uniontown for the service. I will be looking forward to your visit because I am lost without our sister. I know you will give me strength, and your presence will help lift me out of my deep sorrow.

Your loving sister,
Mária

Sisters: Mária Ďurica Ďursa & Anna Ďurica Sopkovich, (Abt 1945)
Youngstown, OH. Authors' archive.

Pisani lis na 22 aprila rok 1953
Slava isusukristu kristos voskres
crasno pozdravisa ot tvojej matere
matere mary ~~Skrilla~~ atoje pretebe mojaluba
tiško justin atvoju fameliju taktipisem želem

"With Grandma": Sharon Zirbes, Grandma (Mary Dursa), Georgette Zirbes, 1950, Youngstown, OH   Author's archive.

douvičisa linemam čapisati lem semaj dobri
rasluči tamaj sedobri mojalubatiško tabut zboham
ajačula žesevital Helenisa
tiško mihvarila joškva kejta   gutbaj XXTXX
                                                        XXXX
                                                         X

22 April, 1953 Youngstown, OH   *Prajeme vám Veselé a štastné Veľkonočné, sviatky.*
(Greetings for a Happy Easter)

Easter Greetings (Kristus voskres) to you, daughter Justina, and to your family.
I received your letter, and your sister Sophie sends you greetings, too.
She was here to visit me and spent one night.

Greetings to your husband and to your daughters.

I cannot go anywhere. I am just sitting home by myself, and I don't even go to church.
I just sit and don't even cook for myself anymore. But it is good that I have my house.

Vera greets you, and I greet you again one hundred times. Please write to me.
That's all and take care.
"Gutbaj" XXXXXXX

Oh, I heard that my granddaughter Helen got married.
Oh, and greetings from your brother Joe and his wife Cate.

Author's note from an Easter card from Slovakia:

Veselú Veľkú noc!
Sladké koláče
Ohybné korbáče
Vodu studenú
Šunku údenú
K tomu veľa zdravíčka.

Happy Easter
Sweet cakes
Flexible whip
Cold water
Smoked Ham
We say many times
Good Health to you.

Author's photo.

Pisane dn 23 oktobra 1953

Slava Isusukristu   Crasnapozdravina

ot tvojej matere Mary. Shirila   atr pretebe moja

lubatipko justin atvoju   Jamelïju tak vas

pozdravujem abitvoje itipki nastoras takti

ž pusem justin žejak semus banepises ajaksipisal

lasi pisala žesichara taotpis žejak filujes bobrat

Misko miehvarel žetibarj taskorobis tanerop

nemušis   etabri jaus

nemožem   eksti pirite

namña   n anidocerkvi

pupmña   žlerndama

lem toten   tapazdravuju

sestri   la schlaparn

margita   ...ocaras ateras ta pazdravujem mojaluba

tipko justin ičovrica itvojutipki nasdaras

tatako tinemam čapi sati lem miotpis nazat

tamajtase tobri domi čira labut zbaham

       justin majaluba tipko   gulbaj XXXXXX

   apazdrag tam helenu i petra gutbaj

23 October, 1953. Youngstown, OH   *Níet ruže bez tŕňa*. (There is no rose without a thorn.)

I am sending one hundred times greetings to you, my daughter Justina, and to your family,
and especially to your two girls. You are not writing to me How do you feel? Please write and
tell me how you are feeling, especially how is your health.

My brother, Michael Dorris, says that you work too hard, so don't work so hard.
He enjoyed his visit with you this past summer in Tinley Park.

Now I am not feeling good. I cannot even cook for myself, and I can't go anywhere.
When are you coming to visit me?

The priest comes to me at home and gives me confession and communion here at home.
My legs hurt so much that it is hard to walk.

Vera and Dutch and family greet you one hundred times, as does Julia, John, and Margie.

My dear daughter, I greet you and your girls once more one hundred times. I hope you
will answer me. Take care of yourself.
"Gutbaj" XXXXXXX to you dear Justina, my dear daughter, and to your sister Helen and Peter.

Author's note:
July, 1954 was Esther's (Justina) last visit to Youngstown and last time to see her mother . After returning home to Tinley Park, IL she suffered increasing lung/breathing problems. On Saturday, August 21, she was visited at home by the priest, Rev. Thomas O'Connell, from St. George's Catholic Church in Tinley Park who administered communion to her. That afternoon she collapsed and was taken by her husband, George, to Hazelcrest Hospital, and at 10:30 p.m. that evening she died. Her death was due to cancer complications from a 1949 diagnosis of breast cancer. She was 49 years old. Her funeral and burial at Holy Sepulchre Cemetery was attended by her friends and family: her husband, her two daughters Sharon and Georgette, her sisters: Sue, Helen, Sophie, Vera, and Julia; her brother Joe and wife Cate Shrilla, and her uncle Mike Dorris from Youngstown. Her mother was not able to attend.
   "Because I could not stop for Death—He kindly stopped for me." (Emily Dickinson)

4732 Raccoon Road, Canfield, OH July, 1954.
Front row: Helen Kostelnik; George, Esther (Justina), Georgette Zirbes.
Back row: son Tom Sopkovich, father Dr. Nick Sopkovich,   son Nick Sopkovich, Jr., and
daughter Joann Sopkovich. Author's archive.

Mary Dursa's Death Certificate

Reg. Dist. No. 50	**OHIO DEPARTMENT OF HEALTH**	State File No.	47009
Primary Reg. Dist. No. 5001	DIVISION OF VITAL STATISTICS	Registrar's No.	
	CERTIFICATE OF DEATH		

1. PLACE OF DEATH

a. COUNTY Mahoning

b. CITY ((If outside corporate limits, write OR RURAL and give township) VILLAGE Youngstown

c. LENGTH OF STAY (in this place)

d. FULL NAME OF HOSPITAL OR INSTITUTION (If NOT in hospital or institution, give street address or location) 722 Steel St.

2. USUAL RESIDENCE (Where deceased lived. If institution, residence before admission.)

a. STATE Ohio

b. COUNTY Mahoning

c. CITY (If outside corporate limits, write RURAL and give township) OR VILLAGE Youngstown

d. STREET (If rural, give location) ADDRESS 722 Steel St.

3. NAME OF DECEASED (TYPE OR PRINT)

a. (First) Mary
b. (Middle)
c. (Last) Dursa

4. DATE OF DEATH (Month) 7 (Day) 3 (Year) 1955

5. SEX F

6. COLOR OR RACE W

7. MARRIED, NEVER MARRIED, WIDOWED, DIVORCED (Specify) Widow

8. DATE OF BIRTH Nov. 20, 1870

9. AGE (In years last birthday) 84 — Under 1 Year Months 7 Days 13 — If Under 24 Hr Hours Min.

10a. USUAL OCCUPATION Housewife

10b. BUSINESS OR INDUSTRY OwnHome

11. BIRTHPLACE (State or foreign country) Porach, Spiska Zupa, Slovakia

12. CITIZEN OF WHAT COUNTRY

13. FATHER'S NAME Michael Duritza

14. MOTHER'S MAIDEN NAME Mary Morosko

15. WAS DECEASED EVER IN U.S. ARMED FORCES? no

16. SOCIAL SECURITY NO. None

17. INFORMANT'S SIGNATURE Joseph Skrivela

18. CAUSE OF DEATH Enter only one cause per line for (a), (b), and (c)

MEDICAL CERTIFICATION

I. DISEASE OR CONDITION DIRECTLY LEADING TO DEATH* (a) Acute Myocarditis — INTERVAL BETWEEN ONSET AND DEATH 5-2-55

ANTECEDENT CAUSES
Morbid conditions, if any, DUE TO (b) Hypertension, Arterio- — 5-2-55
giving rise to the above cause (a) stating the underlying cause last. DUE TO (c) sclerosis, Nephro-sclerosis

II. OTHER SIGNIFICANT CONDITIONS
Conditions contributing to the death but not related to the disease or condition causing death.

19a. DATE OF OPERATION

19b. MAJOR FINDINGS OF OPERATION none 446X

20. AUTOPSY? Yes [ ] No [ ]

21a. ACCIDENT SUICIDE HOMICIDE (Specify)

21b. PLACE OF INJURY (e.g., in or about home, farm, factory, street, office building, forest, etc.)

21c. (CITY, VILLAGE, OR TOWNSHIP) (COUNTY) (STATE)

21d. TIME OF INJURY (Month) (Day) (Year) (Hour) m.

21e. INJURY OCCURRED While at Work [ ] Not While at Work [ ]

21f. HOW DID INJURY OCCUR?

22. I hereby certify that I attended the deceased from _____, 19____, to July 3, 19 55, and that death occurred at 6:00m P.m., from the causes and on the date stated above.

23a. SIGNATURE Walter O. Merwin M.D. (Degree or title)

23b. ADDRESS YOUNGSTOWN

23c. DATE SIGNED 7/12-55

24a. BURIAL, CREMATION, REMOVAL (Specify) Burial

24b. DATE July 7, 55

24c. NAME OF CEMETERY OR CREMATORY St. Mary Cemetery

24d. LOCATION (City, town, or county) (State) Youngstown, Ohio

NAME OF EMBALMER J.G. Vaschak Jr (LIC. NO.) 5037A

25. FUNERAL DIRECTOR'S SIGNATURE Joseph D. Vaschak (LIC. NO.) 3512

FUNERAL FIRM AND ADDRESS J.G. Vaschak Funeral Home 40 Lincoln Ave. Youngstown, Ohio (STREET NO.) (CITY) (STATE)

DATE REC'D BY LOCAL REG.

REGISTRAR'S SIGNATURE J. R. Mellon

SUB-REGISTRAR'S SIGNATURE

July 3, 1955 Death of Mary Dursa

The large Slovak spirit of Mary Dursa, that had borne 12 children, raised 11, plus one nephew, departed her life on July 3, 1955, in Youngstown, Ohio.

"Though our firmament hath lost a light, it shines in other skies for other eyes."

DURSA—Mrs. Mary, 84, of 722 Steel St., died Sunday. She was born Nov. 20, 1870, in Porach, Spiska Zupa, Slovakia, a daughter of Michael and Mary Morosko Duritza. She was a member of St. Mary Greek Catholic Church and the Greek Catholic Union Lodge 543. Her husband, Michael, died 20 years ago. She leaves two sons, Michael Sirilla of Yonkers, N.Y., and Joseph Shirilla of Youngstown: six daughters, Mrs. Katherine Kalich of Uniontown, Pa., Mrs. Sophie Kuchta of Yonkers, Mrs. Helen Kosteinik of Chicago, Miss Sue Sirilla of Hollywood, Calif., Mrs. Vera Pallo and Mrs. Julia Lesnak, both of Youngstown; two brothers, John Duritza of Youngstown and Michael Dorris of Campbell; a sister, Mrs. Helen Dursa of Uniontown: 33 gandchilden and 21 great-gandchildren. Funeral services will be held at 8:30 a.m. Thursday at the residence and 9 a.m. in the church. Interment St. Mary's Greek Catholic Cemetery. Friends may call at the residence any time. VASCHAK FUNERAL HOME.   RI 4-0235

Modlitba Pána	The Lord's Prayer
Otče náš, ktorý si na nebesiach!	Our Father, who art in heaven,
Posväť sa meno tvoje,	Hallowed be Thy name.
Príd' kráľovstvo tvoje,	Thy kingdom come, THY WILL BE DONE.
Buď vôľa tvoja ako v nebi tak i na zemi!	On earth as it is in heaven.
Chlieb náš každodenný daj nám dnes,	Give us this day, our daily bread,
A odpúšť nám naše viny, ako i my odpúšťame svojim vinníkom,	And forgive us our trespasses, As we forgive those who trespass against us.
A neuveď nás do pokušenia	And lead us not into temptation,
Ale zbav nás od zlého.	But deliver us from evil.
Amen.	For Thine is the kingdom, and the power, And the glory, forever and forever. Amen

Poráč, *Širilla archive, 2018.*

Spiš, Author's photo.

Mary Dursa, (Abt 1950). Author's archive.

Moonlight Night
By Joseph von Eichendorf

A breeze traversed the wheatfields,
Soft waves rolled out of sight,
The forests whispered gently
In a clear and starry night.

And my soul spread wide its wings
And flew as it had never flown,
Across the quiet countryside,
As if to take me home.

"Cilem viditsja mi?"
(I think of my homeland?)

By Emily Kubek

My thoughts even now fall on the Carpathians.
On my native land that I cannot forget.
Although in my youth fortune did not smile on me,
And I frequently had to struggle from want
And although over there in the homeland
Things were frequently lacking
Still now the native land remains always dear.
I remember the graves where my father and mother lie
Would it not be better to lie next to them?
My thoughts go unto you, oh native land.
Are the evenings and summers more beautiful over there?
Or does it only seem so? Do I only imagine it?

"Das Gebet"
(Prayer)

By Johanna Spyri (1827-1901)

I needed a kinder heart.
Dear Spirit who dwelled in me
You helped me to live and love and work
And of more service be.
I needed a stronger will.
Oh, Eternal One Divine
You gave me strength and made my thoughts
In harmony with Thine.

(from *Heidi's Children,* p. 198.)

PART FOUR – EPILOGUE

Mary Dursa, (Abt 1950). Lesnak-Toth Archive.

Death is to lose the earth you know, for greater knowing;
To lose the life you have, for greater life;
To leave the friends you loved, for greater loving;
To find a land more kind than home, more large than earth.

By Thomas Wolfe, from *You Can't Go Home Again.*

EPILOGUE: THE IMMIGRANT MOTHER   (Author Unknown)

For all of eternity, America is indebted to the immigrant mother, whether she is Slovak, Polish, Italian, Jewish, German, Russian, English, Greek, Bulgarian, Irish, Slovenian, Croatian, Serbian, or Ukrainian.

Born in the old country, she usually married at a young age the young boy with whom she worked in the fields or the boy down the street. While still a young bride and sometimes with child, she remained and waited while her husband left for America—that distant land filled with the promises of a better life.

The days, months, and sometimes years, passed slowly, while she patiently waited for word from her husband. Finally, when the letter came with the passage fare for the long ship voyage to America, she gathered up her few possessions and children and boarded a ship to join her husband.

She found him working in the steel mills, or brickyards, or iron mines, or coal mines, or on the railroad. She found him living in a shack, shanty, railroad car, or even in a tent. But at least this was a start, a foundation for a new life. Here in America, with her husband at her side, she prepared for the years ahead.

Our country was young; it needed laborers, and she gave five, six or more children. While her husband worked in the bitter cold of winter, or the blistering heat of summer, in ditches laying sewers, or deep in the ground mining coal or iron ore, the mothers worked from early morning to late at night, cooking on a coal stove, washing the clothes by hand with a washboard, and heating the water in a copper tub on the coal stove, while at the same time taking care of the children and in many cases also boarders.

Now, years later, the freshness of young womanhood is gone. By the flickering oil lamp she sews and irons clothes late into the night. She scrimps and saves money to dress her children decently, while she wears an older dress and stays at home. Her children must have an education so that they may be respected and amount to something someday.

Then at last, when her children have grown, as her cup of joy runneth over, we see how want, deprivation, and hardship have taken their toll. Worn out, her bones aching from many ills, she lay in her sick bed, her children around her. She turns to kiss them, to bless them, and then she is gone.

She is the unsung hero and pioneer of America. No statue has been built or sculpture been created to commemorate the immigrant mother.

She, whose breast nurtured us, whose arms raised us, whose ideals inspired us, whose tears washed us clean, and whose devotion saved us, found her place in heaven and sends down her blessing on America for what America has given to her children in this great land.

May the children of America never forget what they owe to that blessed woman, the immigrant mother.
*****

Author's note: Many Slavic newspapers print this essay around Mother's Day. The Slovak paper *Jednota* does the same.
(Maria's legacy was just 4 words: *Čo z teba bude?* (Make something of yourself.)

The Statue of Liberty-Ellis Island Foundation, Inc.

proudly presents this

Official Certificate of Registration

in

THE AMERICAN IMMIGRANT WALL OF HONOR

to officially certify that

MARIA DURICOVA SIRILOVA

who came to America from

SLOVAKIA

is among those courageous men and women who came to this country in search of personal freedom, economic opportunity and a future of hope for their families.

Lee A. Iacocca
The Statue of Liberty-Ellis Island
Foundation, Inc.

LIBERTY
1886·1986

LAST WILL AND TESTAMENT

OF

MARY DURSA

I, MARY DURSA, of the City of Youngstown, County of Mahoning and State of Ohio, being of lawful age and of sound and disposing mind and memory, do make, publish and declare this to be my Last Will and Testament, hereby revoking and annulling any and all Wills by me heretofore made.

ITEM I: I direct that all of my just debts and funeral expenses be paid out of my estate as soon as practicable after the time of my decease. I further direct that I be buried in the Cemetery of ST. MARY'S GREEK CATHOLIC CHURCH, Schenley Avenue, Youngstown,Ohio, in the grave lot I own and in the grave space next to the grave of my deceased husband, MICHAEL DURSA. I have erected a monument on said grave lot on which is inscribed my name and the year of my birth. I direct that my Executor hereinafter named, have the year of my death also inscribed on said monument after my decease. I further direct that my funeral rites be conducted from the ST. MARY'S GREEK CATHOLIC CHURCH, Salt Spring Road, Youngstown,Ohio, of which REV. JOSEPH JACKANICH is now the Pastor. As a part of my funeral expenses, I further direct that the sum of ONE HUNDRED DOLLARS ($100.00) be paid to the Pastor at the time of my decease of ST. MARY'S GREEK CATHOLIC CHURCH, Salt Spring Road, Youngstown,Ohio, for the saying of masses for the repose of my soul and that of my deceased husbands, MICHAEL SHIRILLA and MICHAEL DURSA.

ITEM II: All of the rest, residue and remainder of my estate, real, personal and mixed, of every kind and description whatsoever and wheresoever situated, which I may own and have the right to dispose of at the time of my decease, I give, devise and bequeath unto my children, MICHAEL SHIRILLA, of 22 Jefferson Street, Yonkers, N.Y., JOSEPH SHIRILLA, of 1229 Rigby Street, Youngstown,Ohio, VERONA DURSA PALLO, of Youngstown,Ohio, and JULIA DURSA LESHNAK, of

108

Youngstown, Ohio, absolutely and in fee simple, equally, share and share alike, provided, however, that after my decease they pay the following:

a). To my daughter, KATHERINE DURICA, of Lamont Furnace, Pennsylvania, the sum of TWO HUNDRED FIFTY DOLLARS ($250.00);

b). To my daughter, HELEN KOSTELNIK, of 2055 W. 51st Street, Chicago, Illinois, the sum of TWO HUNDRED FIFTY DOLLARS ($250.00);

c). To my daughter, SOPHIE KUCHTA, of 143 Stanley Ave., Yonkers, N.Y., the sum of TWO HUNDRED FIFTY DOLLARS ($250.00);

d). To my daughter, ESTHER ZIRBES, of 17801 Ridgland, Tinley Park, Illinois, the sum of TWO HUNDRED FIFTY DOLLARS ($250.00);

e). To my daughter, SUZANNE SHIRILLA, of 1131 1/4 N. Bronson, Hollywood, California, the sum of TWO HUNDRED FIFTY DOLLARS ($250.00).

ITEM III: I make no provision for my grandchildren, the children of my deceased daughter, MARY SHIRILLA NOVAK.

ITEM IV: I make, nominate and appoint my son, JOSEPH SHIRILLA, to be the Executor of this my Last Will and Testament, and request that no bond be required of him as such Executor.

IN WITNESS WHEREOF, I have hereunto set my hand at Youngstown, Ohio, this 24th, day of May, 1951.

Mary Dursa

SIGNED by the said MARY DURSA and acknowledged by her to be her Last Will and Testament in our presence, sight and hearing, who at her request have hereunto subscribed our names as witnesses in her presence and in the presence of each other at Youngstown, Ohio, this 24th, day of May, 1951.

Mary E Franks residing at 138 E Judson Ave
Youngstown, Ohio

Arthur N K Friedman residing at 76 Jeannette Drive
Youngstown, Ohio

718 and 722 Steel Street, Youngstown, OH   Lesnak-Toth photo. April, 2018.

 Author's note: The expression "Two cooks can spoil the broth." could apply to the occupants of the house at 722 after Maria's daughter Vera's marriage in 1932, since both mother and daughter had to share one kitchen.   Since this was depression time with significant job loss, Maria probably engaged relatives who were carpenter savvy to build an extension from the existing dining room out to become her own kitchen. Thus she could enjoy cooking her own Slovak favorites, which she was very proud of. This addition was probably a mutual decision between mother and daughter. The photo below from the author's archive was taken about 1940, and one can see evidence of this kitchen addition in the background of the photo.
(You can also see evidence of this addition on the back end of the above 2018 current photo.)
From left to right in the photo below are: Son-in-law Peter Kostelnik, Maria, Sister Anna Sopkovich, Daughter Helen Kostelnik. Author's archive.

110

APPENDIX

QR link to *Slovensko Moje* (My Slovakia) video:

Anna Ziolkovsky, niece of Mária's husband, Mike Sirilla, Poráč, 1985. Author's photos.

END NOTES

Acknowledgments:

My uncle, Michael Sirilla, took me to Slovakia in 1984. While there he introduced me to our Širila relatives in Poráč and our Ďurica relatives in Rudňany, Spišská Nová Ves, Prešov, and Košice. Of enormous help in gaining knowledge of the history of the Ďurica family was my cousin Štefan Cvengroš. To these two remarkable men I have dedicated this book with deepest heartfelt thanks.

Many thanks are due to Norbert Duritza of Chalk Hill, PA, (whose roots are also from Poráč through his grandfather Andrej Durica) who sent me family history research from Nick Duritsa, a grandson of Katherine Sirilla Duritsa, which led me to Shirley Cave Navarro, his cousin. Her details of Katherine's children and their spouses filled the missing piece of that family group.

Many thanks are due to the late Rose Gambone Novak (age 93) for the phone interview on November 14, 2013 for total recall of the names of children and their respective spouses of Mary Sirilla Novak, Rose's former mother-in-law. Rose was married to Mary Novak's only son Joseph Novak. Rose's daughter, Rita, was my initial contact. I also had help from Mike Bell, historian of the Dunbar Historical Society and Mary Catharine Petrosky Sansig of Connellsville, PA, granddaughter of Mary Sirilla Novak. Thanks are also due to Mary Novak's other grandchildren: John Petrosky of ID, Antoinette Petrosky Hickey of FL (especially for her family tree found on ancestry.com), and Joe Petrosky of Denver, CO

Thanks are also due to other cousins who helped verify, correct, and give additions to their respective family groups: Cindy Blick Hecker; Colleen Blick Tierney, who also is the author of the historical fiction, **The Weight of Coal and Lace, the story of Andras and Sophie Kuchta**, 2012; the late George Sirilla; the late Richard Shrilla; June Shrilla Carducci and her mother the late Cate Shrilla whose retellings of family history were my guideposts; Margaret Lesnak Toth, Joanne Pallo Klacik, & Richard Pallo all Youngstown cousins, contributing to family photos and stories; Maureen Peel, granddaughter of John Duritza, brother to Mária, for her photos and remembrances; the late Dorothy Sopkovich Pohmurski, granddaughter of Anna Sopkovich, sister to Mária, for her meticulous and detailed family history from the Youngstown, OH area. Of great help in sorting out various details is due to Thomas and Nick Sopkovich. Thanks to my readers of the manuscript: Claudia Mariani of Thun, Switzerland; Georgette Zirbes, of Ann Arbor, MI; Phoebe Fuller Spichiger, of Hünibach, Switzerland; Alena Polklabová of Poráč, Slovakia; and Nikolov, Marianne of Pécs, Hungary. To my friend and translator of Maria's original letters to her sister Katka in Rudňany and Maria's letters to my mother "Justina" in Tinley Park, IL, I give thanks to Jan Jancosek, an émigré from Smilno, Saris County, Slovakia and current resident of Boulder, CO. Thanks too for the many IT sessions with Lisa Jones and GiGi Nielsen. Yea, for their help!

All of the above family and friends helped me enormously in the compiling of this memoir. However, the sustaining genealogy knowledge and encouragement of my friend and colleague, Fran Caparrelli, of the Bud Werner Memorial Library in Steamboat Springs, CO was unparalled. Her insistence on facts and truth as much as possible is consistent with genealogical writing; the embellishments are, of course, my responsibility. Credit must also be given for the deadlines and listeners of the Genealogy Writing Group. *D'akujeme vam za vaš pomoc.* (Thank you for your help.)

February 15, 1909 Poráč, Dearest Anna
The Košice-Bohumín Railway was started in 1860 and went from Košice along the Hornád River through Markušovce, Spišská Nová Ves, Žilina, Česky Téšín, Bohumín. It was completed by 1871.

A historical summary of names and spellings used for Poráč:
Hungarian=Vereshegy (Vereshhedge) meaning Red Hill.
German= Rotenberg, meaning Red Hill
Polish= Poracz (Porach)
Hungarian=Poracs (Porach)
Slovak=Poráč (Porach)
The population of Poráč in 1900 was 1,800. In 1920 was 880. Today it is about 1,200.

The Jurek Family, of which Katka was the mother, lived in today's Rudňany. Prior to 1948, this small village was called in Slovak Koterbachy and in German Kotterbach. It was the headquarters for the Hungarian Mariassy family. Its population today is 4,246. From 1895 it was well known in the area as the location of the Vitkovické Iron Works, miners of iron ore.

May 1, 1909, Poráč, Dearest Anna
The dates of Maria's Family History are verified from: "Slovak Church and Synagogue Books" from the website www.familysearch.org; and www.@iarelative.com/porac. Microfilms from the LDS Family History Library in Salt Lake City: #1791519; and #1791520 were also used. (See Endnote June 24, 1941 for Maria's birth and baptism documents.)
Michal Širila is found on a passenger list from Ellis Island dated arrival 1887, New York, by the name "Mihaly Schirila," which is the Hungarian spelling. His age is listed as 18. His baptism record lists him born in 1867. On the ship's manifest next to his name are two others whose surnames are common in Poráč: Demeter Mivlik and Matko Galeida. The next passenger list, crossing from Bremen to New York is dated April 7, 1891, for Mihaly Serila. This is before Maria's first child, Maria, was born. In the Appendix is also Michael's and Maria's separate passenger lists for 1896 found on www.ancestry.com

The family story states that Michael went to work in the coal mines in Hubbard, Ohio which opened in the late 1860s. It is also stated in Štefan Hanuščin's book *Poráč* that from 1880-1890 the mines in Poráč were closed. A family story told that an uncle, a Cvengroš, was already in the US working in Hubbard. Recruiters went to small villages in eastern Slovakia where men had some experience in mining. The mine owners in the US wanted workers who did not speak English because they could not easily complain about the horrible working conditions and low pay. They also preferred men who could not read or write. Girls were recruited, too, to live at the local priest's residence and clean (as servants) and cook for the local priest. The Ellis Island records show incoming arrivals. Outgoing (those returning to Europe) records are very minimal. Persons who left illegally, without a passport or an emigration permit, were often identified by local police at the port of departure. This could explain why Michael Sirilla on the manifest of his second passage is recorded as "female." The family story is that he had to dress as a woman to get ship passage to New York. There is today phone record evidence of both surnames Sirilla and Cvengroš in Hubbard, OH. More information can be acquired from the Hubbard Public Library, Reference Desk.

The "Slovensko" stamps are copies of papercuts by the Czech artist, Kornelie Némecková, in the 1980s, Prague, Czech Republic.

September 7, 1909 New York, USA Dearest Katka
The *Bremen* crossed the Atlantic in 10 days, however, seasickness and boredom were the biggest problems. Passengers would only say in almost delirium, "Sky and water, nothing but sky and water." After 1900 the number of passengers leaving Bremen was about 250,000 a year. (From *Destination*

America, published by Temmen ,Bremen,2014.) The ship's manifest record for Maria Sirila, her 5 children, and her sister Helena was found on the Family History Library microfilm #1400014, Bremen to New York, 1909. Between 1892 and 1920 over 12 million emigrants went through Ellis Island.

In the reference book, *The Mark Twain Encyclopedia*, by J.R. LeMaster, 1993, p. 28, "Someone said that Mark Twain had sailed on the ship *Bremen*, in 1907, when he returned to the US from a speaking tour in Europe."

August 1, 1910, Lemont Furnace, PA Dearest Katka
Maria Sirilla and Michael Dursa were married by the priest from St. Mary's Assumption Greek Catholic Church in New Salem, PA. The cornerstone for this church was laid in 1903 and was written in Slovak. Michael Dursa's first wife, Maria Dursa, is listed as deceased as of Feb, 1907 as stated on the application for his second marriage to Maria Sirilla. However no death certificate can be found and therefore no correct maiden name is known. She probably is buried in the St. Stephen's cemetery in Leisenring, PA

"It's not that you are in the story, it's the story in you."   According to Shirley Cave Navarro, granddaughter of Katharine Duritsa, the people in the photo are in front of the Gulcher half of the duplex in Lemont Furnace. The other half was that of John Duritsa and his wife Katharine, and it formerly housed Maria and Michael Sirilla and their 9 children before Michael's death in 1908.

September 8, 1915, Star Junction, PA Dearest Katka
By 1902 a Pennsylvania law said that boys had to be at least age 12 in order to work as a breaker boy and had to be at least age 14 to work underground.   Most boys who worked as a breaker boy were between the ages of 8-12 years old. Parents would lie about their child's age.

The newspaper, *Slovák v Amerike*, founded in Pittsburgh in 1886 stated that in 1908 the national Child Labor Committee estimated that 1 out of every 4 mine workers was a boy from the age of 7-16. The younger boys usually worked as breaker boys. At the age of 14 supposedly it was legal for a boy to go down into the mine. However, many parents overstated their son's age in order to have him earn more money by working underground earlier than age 14.

In 1938, President Roosevelt signed into law the **Fair Labor Standards Act**, (FLSA) which the Supreme Court ruled constitutional in 1941. It stated that a child must be at least age 16 to work on most jobs that are not hazardous; farming was excepted.

In 1969, the United Mine Workers, the union for coal miners, convinced the U.S. Congress to enact the landmark legislation called the **Federal Coal Mine Health and Safety Act**, which provided compensation for miners suffering from black lung disease (*pneumoconiosis*) and compensation to family survivors. This was through the Department of Labor.

December 22, 1918, Star Junction, PA Dearest Katka
Vianočné Koledy (Slovak Christmas carols)   can be accessed at: www.vianoce.sk/18911-koledy-historia.php   Also additional information on Slovak Christmas traditions can be found at: www.slovakheritage.org

Christmas decorations in Slovakia usually remain in tact through January 6, the Christian holiday called Epiphany, or the Feast of the Three Kings. This day commemorates the arrival of the three wise men from the East who were led by a star to the Infant Jesus in Bethlehem: Caspar, Melchior, and Balthasar.

Many children in small villages still dress up as the three kings and go from house to house singing carols and being presented with sweets.

January 22, 1919, Star Junction, PA Dearest Katka
The Pittsburgh Agreement was drafted and signed in the Loyal Order of Moose Building in Pittsburgh on May 31, 1918 by Tomáš Masaryk and representatives of émigré American Slovak and Czech fraternal groups. The Pittsurgh area included the largest concentration of Slovaks outside of Slovakia.   The new country of Czecho-Slovakia would stretch 600 miles, from northwestern Bohemia through Moravia, through Slovakia, and included western Ruthenia. The hyphen in the name symbolized the autonomy that Slovakia would be granted for the official use of the Slovak language in schools and government affairs.   The hyphen was later removed and the country was called "Czechoslovakia," signifying the power of the politicians in the capital of Prague. Ruthenia was later grabbed by Hungary.

On September 9, 2007, the *original* document of this Pittsburgh Agreement was donated by the Slovak League of America to the permanent collection of the John Heinz History Center in Pittsburgh.

Father Alexander Dzubay was the founder of St. Stephen's Greek Catholic Church in Leisenring, Pennsylvania. He was born in Kalnik, Berezhanets, Hungary (Podkarpatskarus) on February 17, 1857 and later studied at the gymnasium in Užhorod, having graduated in 1880. Upon his emigration to the US, his first church was the Greek Catholic Church in Wilkes-Barre, Pennsylvania. In 1892 he was assigned to establish St Stephen's Greek Catholic Church in Leisenring. He baptized all of the children of Michael and Maria Sirilla.

"Tót" is a slur word used by Hungarians to refer to Slovaks, and it may have originated from the German word "tot" which literally means "dead." The Hungarians liked to use the phase "Tót nem ember" to cause insult to a Slovak's pride, translating to "Slovaks are not human." Other references used by Hungarians toward Slovaks are words for: scum, ignorant, dull, or impoverished.   Should one hear these words today by Hungarian nationalists, it navigates perfectly into "Let's make Hungary great again!"

Slovak immigrant workers in the US were usually referred to as "Hunkies," meaning those emigrating from the political unit of Hungary, part of the dual country of Austria-Hungary.   Many emigres put "Austria" on their passenger manifest as their country of origin, instead of Hungary. On the 1920 census Slovaks said the country of birth was "Slovakland."

August 18, 1919, Star Junction, PA Dearest Katka
The Homestead Act was signed by President Lincoln on May 20, 1862 and allowed the head of a household to file for 160 acres, build a house, clear forty acres, make other improvements, and live on the property for 5 years. The act did allow the homesteader to sell his rights before the 5 years were up. Some filed and stayed long enough to sell their claim, or part of it, move on, and repeat the game of land speculation. The 40 acres bought by Eliáš Dyuritza and the 120 acres bought by his brother-in-law, Mathias Nemscik, together made up one homestead, 160 acres, evidence that the original was subdivided. Maria's brother-in-law, John Shirilla, bought 40 acres of a homestead near Eliáš Dyuritza's land. (The photo of John is included to show possible resemblance to his brother Michael Sirilla.) This area of midwestern Minnesota was said to have the most fertile land in the whole state.

Helen Dyuritza, wife of Eliáš Dyuritza and mother of three young children: Julia (6), Esther (4), and baby Michael (7 months), died on May 30, 1916 of mental complications in the mental hospital in Fergus

Falls, Minnesota. For more details, the complete newspaper article dated June 1, 1916 from the Fergus Falls weekly gazetteer can be obtained from the Historical Society of Fergus Falls, Otter Tail County, MN, or viewed on the Sirila Tree at www.ancestry.com

Eliáš Dyuritza died on August 12, 1919 in Monesson, PA and his will was executed on June 23, 1919 prior to his death. He bequeathed his 103 and ½ acres (increased from the original 40) in Todd County, Minnesota, part of Section 34, to his children: Julia, Esther, and Michael. He appointed his brother, John Duritza, of Star Junction, PA as executor of his will and guardian of his children. Eliáš was also known by a nickname of Alec. This could have originated in Poráč, where siblings might have called him by the Hungarian name "Elek," which later became "Alec" in the U.S. In the 1900 census, he and his wife are recorded as living with his sister Maria and her husband Michael Sirilla in Lemont, PA, and they are listed in the household as "Alec and Ella." It should have been Eliáš and Helen.

June 18, 1920 Star Junction, PA Dearest Katka
Young Steve Dursa's tragic death was a story told many times by members of the Dursa family. His biological mother died in February, 1907, which is on the remarriage application of Michael Dursa and Maria Sirilla.

July 11. 1922, Star Junction, PA   Dearest Katka
Joseph Sirilla, second son of Maria, enlisted in the Army on July 30, 1919 at Pittsburgh, PA and was discharged on July 29, 1922 in Ft. Logan, CO, as "honest and faithful" in the **38th US Army** Infantry division. (The family story is that he also enlisted during WWI under an alias name because his mother would not sign for him.) According to his daughter, June Shrilla Carducci, some of the second enlistment was spent on duty in Vladivostok, Russia, the easternmost Russian city and port on the Pacific Ocean. The only file available at the NARA archives in St. Louis on Joseph Sirilla is the discharge paper due to a fire there in 1973. Currently there is no way to document the division he went to immediately after enlistment. It is conceivable that Joseph could have been active in the **27th US Army** division initially which sent US soldiers to Siberia to aid in the departure of the Czech and Slovak Legion from Vladivostok. This "Legion" consisted of Czechs and Slovaks who defected from the Austrian Hapsburg Army that was fighting against the Russians. The Legion took on the maintenance of the Trans Siberian Railway (which was being sabotaged by the Bolsheviks), as well as aiding Russians not in favor of the Bolsheviks to leave the country through the port of Vladivostok. Joseph's fluency in the Slovak language would have attested to his qualifications. It is said that Slovak fraternals and churches in the US sent out "recruitment" ads for young Slovak men to enlist with the hopes that the US military would utilize their Slovak language expertise and send them to Vladivostok. The 27th and 31st American Infantry divisions were sent to help end violence in Siberia and restore peace and protect democracy. In Masaryk's memoir, **The *Making of a State,*** he states (p. 282) "We have to thank the friendliness of the Allies who lent us ships and soldiers to make the evacuation complete by November 30, 1920." (The Czech and Slovak troops returned to Europe via San Diego, CA and the US.) Masaryk, being a politician, believed that this army, the Czech and Slovak Legion, would alight world countries to his cause for the unification of Czechs and Slovaks into the country called Czechoslovakia, which did materialize officially on October 28, 1918. *The Czech and Slovak Legion in Siberia 1917-1922* by Joan McGuire Mohr, 2012 is recommended reading. The film *The Story Behind the Accidental Army: the Amazing True Story of the Czechoslovak Legion* is also now available.

John Duritza, brother of Maria, moved to Youngstown, about 1922, and worked as a machinist for Republic Steel there. Prior to this move he had a farm in Herbert, Pennsylvania, Fayette County, and kept his coal mining job while his wife, Katharine, and all of his children helped out on the farm. In the photo, Helen, one of his daughters and Esther, his niece (orphaned daughter from his deceased brother Eliáš) are pictured at the farm. Both Helen and Esther, cousins, had the same birthdays, June 11, 1912. After retirement in the 1960s, John and his wife Katharine moved to Tuscon, Arizona where his daughter, Helen Duritza Steffen and her family lived.   John and Katharine later divorced.

Feather stripping, called *páračky* (pronounced paa-raach-kee) was a common winter activity in Slovakia for making a feather quilt as part of a young daughter's dowry, and in the US for making a feather quilt to keep warm! Down feathers were used for pillows, and the stripped feathers were used for the quilts.

Anna Sopkovich benefited from what was called prior to 1922 as "naturalization by marriage" benefit for women who were married to aliens who became naturalized. Anna's husband, Joseph, was naturalized in 1900. This benefit also applied to dependent children.   This benefit was negated by the Cable Act of 1922 which stated that a woman had to apply for her own naturalization, whether married or not, and could not acquire automatically naturalization from the husband's new citizenship.

August 1, 1924 Youngstown, OH Dearest Katka
The first steel in Youngstown was made in 1892 at what was called the Ohio Steel Company. It merged in 1899 with the National Steel Company of Pittsburgh, and in 1901 that merger was with the Carnegie Steel Company which later became the Ohio Works of US Steel. Youngstown Sheet and Tube, Republic Steel Company, and Youngstown Ice Company were also big steel producers in the Youngstown area. There always existed serious hazards for workers: chemical explosions, extreme heat, unshielded equipment and usually 12 hour work days. Income usually amounted for workers to about $500 a year. The depression hit hard in Youngstown, and by 1933 one third of steel workers were unemployed. By 1939 some of the mills started producing war materials. See *Youngstown and the Mahoning Valley.* Today there is only clean air and no producing steel mills.

Maria's niece Julia Dyuritza was committed to the mental hospital in Massillon, OH sometime in the 1920s, however the current facility called Heartland Behavioral Healthcare Organization, in Massillon, will not release any records. There exists a photo of Julia with her sister Esther in Michigan (courtesy of Maureen Peel) so it is assumed that she was released from the facility and was in the custody of her sister Esther sometime after the death of Esther's husband.   Julia's death certificate states the place of death as Eastpointe, Michigan on September 18, 1994, with burial at Evergreen Cemetery, Detroit, Michigan. She was 84 at the time of death. Dorothy Sopkovich Pohmurski writes that a group of family visited Julia in approximately 1948 at the hospital in Massillon, Ohio. Her address at that time was Unit C, Box 540, 44646. According to Dorothy, in 1946 Anna Sopkovich received a letter from Julia, sent from the hospital at Massillon, Ohio.

The Johnson-Reed Act was passed on May 26, 1924 and stated that immigration from any country was limited to 2% of the number of citzens from any country based on the 1890 census, restricting immigration from southern and eastern Europe and negating peoples from Italy, Slavic nations, eastern European Jews, Africans, Middle Easterners, and barring Asians entirely. Thus 86% of people admitted after 1924 were from northern European countries. These restrictions were lifted by the Nationality & Immigration Act of 1965.

August 1, 1925, Youngstown, OH Dearest Katka
Jane Addams, the founder of Chicago's Hull House said, "Never before in civilization have such numbers of young girls been suddenly released from the protection of the home and permitted to walk

unattended upon the city streets and to work under alien roofs." In Carl Sandberg's famous poem, "Chicago," he states, "They tell me you are wicked and I believe them, for I have seen your painted women under the gas lamps luring the farm boys. And they tell me you are brutal and my reply is: on the faces of women and children I have seen the marks of wanton hunger………. however, Chicago is proud to be the Hog butcher for the World, Tool Maker, Stacker of Wheat, Player with Railroads and the Nation's Freight Handler; stormy, husky, brawling, city of the big Shoulders."

November 30, 1931 Youngstown OH Dearest Katka
Esther and George were married on October 7, 1934 in Crown Point, Indiana. This was a very popular place for Chicago area couples to elope to and be married by a Justice of the Peace. It became the "in" thing to do at that time. On the newspaper death notice of Michael Dursa, dated October 23, 1934 Esther is named "Esther Sirilla." Either the family did not yet know that she was married, or it was a family error by the informer, Mary Dursa, Esther's mother. Esther never drove a car.

Maria Dursa could have studied from her elementary school days in Poráč about the Spišská Nová Ves' Protestant minister by the name of Jonás Andrej Czirbesz (Hungarian spelling) (1732-1813) who was the first person to summit the fourth highest peak of the Tatra Mountains called Kriváň on August 4, 1773. In Duncan Gardiner's ***German Towns in Slovakia***, many towns in Spiš were originally settled by Germans from the Rhineland, and he sites a town originally named Bauschendorf (today called Bušovse) located in northern Spiš founded in 1345 which has the uncanny spelling similarity to George Zirbes' father's ancestral village called Bausendorf, which is located along the Mosel River midway between Trier and Koblenz in the Rhineland part of Germany. It is interesting to find this German surname Zirbes in the area of Spišská Nová Ves.

June 24, 1941, Youngstown OH Dearest Katka
Mary Dursa's date of birth on both the Petition for Naturalization and the Declaration of Intention is listed as December 23, 1871. This is inaccurate according to two reliable sources:
l. The birth record from St. Demeter's Greek Catholic Church in Poráč, Slovakia lists her birth as November 20, 1871. Her father's name is Michal Gyurisza; her mother's name is Mária Mrozko.
Online source is "Slovak Church and Synagogue Records" from www.familysearch.org

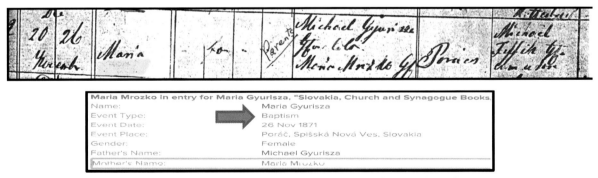

2. The birth record from the address book of Mary's daughter, Esther Sirilla Zirbes:

Birthdays: Dec. 14 Susanne   May 28 Vera   Oct. 6 Michael
           Mar. 7 Sophie   Jul. 16 Helen   ****Nov. 20 Mother
           Apr. 13 Julia   Mar. 16 Esther

The Smith Act was signed into law by President Roosevelt on June 28, 1940. As a war grew more likely, the Federal government viewed its alien population as a security concern, so the Smith Act made it compulsory for all aliens in the US to complete registration at their local post office, including fingerprinting. In return, the alien would receive a registration card by mail. After the U.S. declared war in December,1941, 2,971 residents in the U.S. of enemy nations were identified through the Alien Registration program (Smith Act) and taken into custody. This was especially targeted at Nazi, Communist, and Japanese sympathizers.

Naturalization required taking an oath of allegiance that disavowed allegiance to any foreign power's leaders; it required demonstrating good character using personal references; and it necessitated having a specified period of residency in the U.S. At this time a non- English-speaking candidate could take the final test in the native language, as long as he/she met the above requirements.

(Author's note) The Hungarian spelling of Maria's father's name does not denote his ethnicity. The spelling only denotes the politics (i.e. Hungary) of the year 1871 in Spiš.

April 5, 1945, Youngstown, OH Dearest Katka

The attack on Pearl Harbor was December 7, 1941, and the end of WWII was September 2, 1945 with the Japanese surrender. The following information was found through U.S. World War II Navy Muster Rolls, 1938-1949, online through www.ancestry.com

Kuchta, Michael: Navy. Service number 650 79 57, Transferred from *USS Matagorda* on July 6, 1943 to the *NAS Trinidad*. Served on the *USS Cecil*, leaving on December 3, 1944 from Oakland, California to Pearl Harbor.

Kuchta, Joseph: Navy. Service number 207 01-05, date of enlistment: Sept 20, 1939, served on the *USS Minneapolis*.

Dyuritza, Michael: Navy. Service number 311 38 05, date of enlistment: December 4, 1939 from Detroit, MI Served on the *USS Quincy* ending February 29, 1940; Served on the *USS Santa Fe*, April 13, 1942, stationed in Pearl Harbor until March 22, 1943. Later he served in the Marshall Islands and the Philippines and assisted in the occupation of Japan on the islands of N. Honshu and Hokkaido.

Not pictured is

Andrew Kuchta: Army. Enlistment March 18, 1941 and served in the Philippines as a Warrant Officer, Private 1st class.

The Slovak National Uprising (*Slovenské Národné Povstanie*, commonly referred to as SNP), an armed resistance to German occupation of Slovakia, began on August 29, 1944, with headquarters in the central Slovak city of Banská Bystrica. The goals of the uprising were to contribute to the defeat of fascism and to renew the previous political union of the Slovaks with the Czechs, which the Germans had destroyed by occupying Prague. Both a Soviet and Anglo-American mission were active with the Slovak partisans. However, the German army was considerably more experienced and they occupied the headquarters at Banská Bystrica by October 27. 1944, capturing almost 20,000 Slovak partisans, many of whom were murdered or taken to concentration camps. *World War II: OSS Tragedy in Slovakia,* by Jim Downs, 2002, is a detailed explanation of the American intelligence operation connected with the Slovak National Uprising. American planes flew in supplies to partisans from Bari Air Force Base in Bari, Italy. *Maria Gulovich, OSS Heroine of World War II,* by Sonya N. Jason, 2009 is an illuminating biography about a Slovak woman who guided American and British intelligence officers in the Tatra Mountains after the surrender, with the goal of capturing escaping German soldiers.

Josef Tiso (1887-1947), president of the independent state of Slovakia from 1939-1945 (or as the Allies called Slovakia a puppet state of Hitler) was responsible for (1) the Slovak army fighting along with the Germans against Poland and the Soviet Union, (2) the persecution of Jews living in Slovakia, (3) the elimination of human rights, and (4) the cooperation of the Slovak government with Germany in the destruction of the Slovak National Uprising. Tiso escaped to Austria in April of 1945 but later was captured and released by American authorities to the reinstated government of Czechoslovakia in Prague where he was placed in jail. His trial was held in Bratislava, and he was convicted of treason for cooperating with the Germans during 1939-1945. After appeals (because he was a priest) were denied, he was hanged on April 18, 1947 in the old town of Bratislava. Even today, there is still controversy about this sentence.

September 30, 1945, Youngstown,OH Dearest Katka
Béla Bartók, the famous Hungarian composer, was an ardent collector of folksongs in the neighboring countries surrounding Hungary. Between 1922-1928 he presented his 3,000+ collection of Slovak folk songs to Matica Slovenska, and it was published as *Slovenské Ľudové Piesne* (Slovak Folk Songs). In the *Naked Face of Genius,* he comments on his research with the Slovaks on p. 330, "The very remoteness that separates these places from civilization made my collecting so much easier than any place else. The open responsiveness of the people and their cooperation so warmly offered eased every step of the way." Bartok's mother was from Martin, Slovakia, and he studied in Bratislava (known as Poszony at the time) from 1894-1899. He loved hiking in the Tatra Mountains. The Slovak folk singing group from Porác can be reached at: www.youtube.com/watch?v=BrQjpav8wEw8t=74s

June 1, 1946, Youngstown, OH Dearest Katka
The classic historic description of Pozdišovce pottery is found in *Pozdišovské Hrnčiarstvo* by Ester Plickova, 1959: Bratislava, Slovakia. Originally the pottery was housed in the 1648 Renaissance mansion of the Sirmajovcov Family. After WWII, the socialist government made it a cooperative owned by the state. The pottery today is led by Jan Poprik. The mayor Jan Cizmarik can be reached at ocu.pozdisovce@inmail.sk (Okres Michalovce, Slovakia 07201).

Anna Matej was a neighbor of Mária's and lived down the street on Steel Street in Youngstown. She was one of two signatures on Maria's "Affidavit of Witness" on Maria's naturalization papers.

The film **The Final Mission** by Slovak filmmaker Dušan Hudec, about American airmen shot down over Slovakia during WWII and taken in by Slovak villagers, was shown in Youngstown, Ohio, spring, 2016. Contact person is Loretta Ekoniak, who can be reached at loretta.ekoniak@gmail.com

January 24, 1947, Youngstown, OH Dearest Katka
The recipe for "orechovník" (walnut roll cake) is from the author's family archive of Esther Zirbes.

April 1, 1947, Youngstown, OH Dearest Katarína (in memory of Katka) *Posviacku obnoveného Sv. Demetria.* (Church service at St. Demetrius Church, Poráč) www.youtube.com/watch?v=ic70_mkLOFI

October 23, 1953, Youngstown, OH Dearest Justina
Nicholas J. Sopkovich (1909-1990) was the first child of all of the Ďurica/Mrosko émigrés' children to obtain a degree in higher education. He graduated from the University of Pittsburgh School of Dental Medicine in 1932 and practiced dentistry in Youngstown for 53 years. He leaves two sons, Nicholas and Thomas, who both practiced dentistry.

July 3, 1955, Youngstown, OH
Mary Dursa died at age 85. She is buried in the cemetery of St. Mary's Greek Catholic Church, Youngstown, OH

THE FAMILY LINEAGE

Mária Durica married **Michal Sirila** in Poráč, Slovakia (then Hungary) in 1890, widowed in 1908, and remarried **Michael Dursa** in New Salem, Pennsylvania in 1910. She raised 9 Sirilla children and 2 Dursa children.

"Memory is a responsibility. 99% of life belongs to the living, and only 1% belongs to the memory of the deceased. Writing is the means of showing the best or most important things of history."
(Arnost Lustig, Czech writer of the 20th century.)

This compilation of data of Mária's children consists of **2** generations and cites just some of the details of the lives of her children, their spouses, and her grandchildren.

I   **Mária (Mary) Sirilla** m. Ján (John) Novak
                (1891--1918)   (17 Jan 1884--13 Jun 1961)

on 30 Jul 1906 at St. John the Baptist Byzantine Church, Uniontown, PA
Mary died in the influenza epidemic of 1918 and was buried in the cemetery of St. Stephen's Greek Catholic Church in Leisenring, PA
She left 5 living children:
Anna (1908 -Abt 1925) m. Andrew Graciana
Steven (15 Feb 1911 – 01 Mar 1911)
Joseph A. (18 May 1912 – 16 Feb 1986) m. Rose Gambone (1920-2016)
Ellen (26 May 1913 - 11 Sep 1913)
Mary H. (11 Jul 1914 – Feb 1984) m. Charles Bodkin
Susan E (04 Oct 1915 – 13 Apr 2006) m. John Rabatin
Mary Catharine (1917-2009) m. Joseph Anthony Petrosky
John Novak, a coal miner, was born in the village of Švábovce east of Poprad, Slovakia, and remarried Anna Shuba, (Abt 1922) a widow with one child, Steven (1908). They lived in Dunbar, PA and had two children together:
Paul A. (29 Jun 1923 – Nov 1971)
Frank E. (28 Feb 1926 – 09 Oct 1996)

II   **Katharine (Katie) Sirilla** m. Ján (John) Duritsa
                (1892-1956)   (27 Jun 1885--01 Dec 1945)
                on 14 Sep 1908 at St. Stephen's Greek Catholic Church, Leisenring, PA

John was born in Poráč; his parents were Juraj Gyurica and Anna Vrabal.
Katie & John lived in Lemont Furnace, PA and 6 children were born there.
Children:
George (06 May 1910–21 Jun 1998) died in Warrenton,VA m. Melinda Petitt
John (17 Feb 1912–23 Dec 1978) died in Forest Park, IL m. Violet Heurter
Ann (13 Feb 1914—01 Jul 1993) died in Dyer, IN m. Marion Edward Cave
Stephen (17 Jan 1917–23 Nov 1918) died in Lemont, PA of influenza .
Nicholas (02 Dec 1920–30 Apr 1986) died in Uniontown, PA m. Anna Simco
Helen (18 Nov 1922--24 Nov 2001) died in Westville, IL m. Andy Lucas
Katie remarried Anton (Andy) Kalich (08 Sep 1888--Mar 1979) in Lemont , PA

III   **Sophie (Sis, Cookie) Sirilla**   m. Andrew (Andy) Kuchta

                (1897-1967)   (07 Dec 1888--02 Jun 1974)

m. in 1915, Leisenring, PA

Andy was born in Serednie, a small town between Užhorod and Mukačevo, in today's Ukraine, an ethnic Ruthenian (Rusyn). He emigrated to the US in 1904 and worked as a coal miner for the Washington Coal & Coke Co in Star Junction, PA where he met Sophie Sirilla His brother John had a grocery store in Yonkers, NY

Andy and Sophie lived in Star Junction and Vanderbilt, PA where their children were born, and they moved to Yonkers, NY (Abt 1925) where they owned a grocery store at 143 Stanley Ave.

Children:

Joseph (Joe) (13 Dec 1915--15 Feb 2010) m. Olga Wiskup on 21 Sep 1946 in North Bergen, NJ. He served in the US Navy in WWII from 1942-1945.

Elizabeth (Bette) (15 Oct 1917–07 Oct 2013) died in Sarasota FL m. Collin Blick (06 Apr 1916--28 Jan 1991) on 11 Jun 1944. He served in the US Coast Guard in WWII.

Andrew George (Andy) (30 Apr 1919-- 21 Mar 1992) He served in the US Army in WWII. He was married to Marie, who was from Ireland.

Michael (Mickey) (25 Nov 1922 – 19 Jan 2001) He served in the US Navy in WWII. He never married.

Margaret (31 Jan 1924-Living) m. John Joseph Cleary, 10 Jun 1945 who served in the US Army Air Corps in WWII.

IV   **Michael (Mike) Sirilla**   m. Helen Sohanage

                (1898 -1995)   (10 Apr 1901-18 Mar 1980)

m. on 20 Oct 1923 in Perryopolis, PA Their 2 children were born in Vanderbilt. They later moved to Yonkers, NY where Mike worked as a mechanic.

As retirees Mike and Helen moved to Perryopolis, and lived at 103 Constitution Av.

Children:

Esther (01 May 1925 Vanderbilt, PA-Aug 1992) was a secretary for member of US Congress. m. George Hickey

George (01 May 1929 Vanderbilt, PA-28 Oct 2015) was a Jesuit seminarian and patent attorney in D.C. m. Floranne Zalewski

V   **Joseph (Joe) Sirilla**   m. Catharine Dzurilla

                (1900 – 1973)   (18 Nov 1900–06 Jan 2000)

m. on 24 Jun 1925 in Perryopolis, PA Catharine was born in Spišský Hrhov, Slovakia. She and Joe later moved to 1229 Rigby St., Youngstown, OH

Joe was a "jack of all trades" but was a mechanic for the railroad for most of his career, with free travel passes to see the US. He served in the US Army from 1919-1922 (38th Infantry Division) including time stationed in Vladivostok, Russia helping the Czech & Slovak Legion maintain the Trans-Siberian Railway.

Children:

June Marie (30 Jun 1929 Youngstown, OH– Living) was a teacher in Catholic schools in Illinois. m. Gene Carducci (08 Oct 1923--14 Jun 2003) on 30 Jul 1940 in Youngstown. He was born in Italy.

Richard J. (07 Feb 1931, Youngstown, OH – 10 Nov 2017) was an orthodontist in Mansfield, OH m. Lorraine Whitaker (12 Jul 1933 – Living) on 09 Jul 1955 in Mt. Gilead, OH

VI   **Anna Sirilla**

(1902-1918) Anna died on 21 Nov 1918 of the influenza and was buried at Hopwood Cemetery, Uniontown, PA She was newly married to Stephen Odiške, a coal miner, who worked for H.C. Frick & Co. in Lemont Furnace, PA They had no children.

VII   **Helen Sirilla**   m.   Alex Conrad

(1903-2002)   (1892–31 Jan 1929)

m. on 29 Sep 1919 in St. Nicholas Greek Catholic Church, Perryopolis, PA
They moved to Youngstown, OH where Alex was employed and later moved to Chicago, IL where they lived at 1812 S. Fisk St.
Alex Conrad died of a sudden appendectomy on 31 Jan 1929.
Children:
Helen (Honey) (01 Feb 1921 in Ohio – 15 Apr 2017)
m. Dominic Licastro (16 Mar 1916--21 Jul 2001) in Chicago on 19 Jan 1955.
Together they had a wedding business; he did the printing, she did the fashion.
Later they moved to 823 N. June St. Los Angeles, CA
John (Jack) (13 Feb 1924 in Chicago– 14 Jun 1979) was a sales executive for a glass company. m. Adaline Frankiewicz on 30 Jun 1955, in Chicago. He served in the US Navy from 1943-1946.

In 1932 Helen remarried Peter Kostelnik (18 Mar 1902--25 Sep 1976) who was also widowed with twin girls, Annabelle & Marie. They lived at 5347 S. Rockwell St., Chicago where they had several different businesses downstairs: grocery, beauty salon, tavern, and they resided upstairs. They later moved to Hollywood, FL where they owned a motel and where Peter died. Helen later resided with her daughter Helen at 823 ½ June St. in Los Angeles, CA
Children:
Lillian (12 Feb 1934 Chicago–Living) m. Bill Valentine (1934--2018) on 27 Feb 1953.

VIII   **Esther Justine Sirilla**   m.   George Peter Zirbes

(1905-1954)   (16 Jan 1899 in Chicago—18 Jan 1962 in San Carlos, CA)

m. on 07 Oct 1934 in Crown Point , IN where they eloped. His parents emigrated from Germany: the father from Bausendorf, Rhineland province, Germany and the mother from Aniela in the Nedze River valley in Posen, Prussia. The mother belonged to the Evangelical Immanuel Lutheran Church at 46th Dearborn St. in Chicago .
Esther and George lived at 5556 W. Kedzie Ave., Chicago. In 1941 they moved to 17801 Ridgeland Ave., Tinley Park, IL where they bought a "farmette," 3 acres, 3 bedroom house, and a chicken coop! George worked 37 yrs. for R. R. Donnelly Printing Co in Chicago. Esther recreated the "Slovak Patch"; vegetable patch, berry patch, fruit patch & plenty of pigs, turkeys, chickens, geese, ducks.

Children:
Sharon Esther (26 Sep 1936, Chicago – Living) was a teacher, librarian, RPCV, Hungary. m. James E. Fuller in Denver CO on 01 Feb 1961. Divor. 16 Mar 1979.
Georgette Marie (03 Sep 1940, Chicago – Living) Professor Emerita of the School of Art & Design, University of Michigan, Ann Arbor. m. Robert J. Stull in Kyoto, Japan on 22 Jul 1965. Divor. 15 Dec. 1971 .

IX  **Nicholas Sirilla** (not pictured)
(15 Nov 1906--18 Jan 1907) died at 2 months from "inanition," insufficient nutrition. He is buried in the cemetery of St. Stephen's Greek Catholic Church, Leisenring, PA

X **Suzanne Sirilla** (1907-1995) never married. Worked as a secretary in NY, CA, FL

XI **Veronika (Vera) Dursa** m. John Matthew (Dutch) Pallo
(1911-2001) (21 Mar 1904--29 Nov 1970)
m. on 31 Sep 1932 in Youngstown, OH They eloped because he belonged to the Lutheran faith. (Her baptism states "Verona" as her first name.) They lived at 722 Steel St. Youngstown, OH Matthew was a machinist at the Youngstown Foundry. His father emigrated from Gemer province, Slovakia and was a founding member of St. John's Evangelical Lutheran Church in Youngstown.
Children:
Joanne (08 May 1933 Youngstown--Living) m. John Klacik (18 Apr 1933--Living) on 03 Jul 1954 in Youngstown. She worked as a med. asst. for a pediatrician.
Matthew (Boots) (13 Mar 1935, Youngstown--14 Aug 2004) was a career Marine serving two tours in Vietnam with numerous medals for bravery. m. Patty De Roberts on 09 Feb 1957 and later was divorced. She died in 1983. He died in Woodbridge, VA
Richard (23 Jan 1937, Youngstown--Living) was a banker. m. Mylove Craft on 28 Apr 1962 and they lived in Woodbridge VA then moved to Sarasota, FL
Michael G. (06 Apr 1947, Youngstown--Living). Was a career marine and a public school teacher. m. Nancy Braidich on 18 Aug 1969. They lived in Woodbridge VA

XII **Julia (Jay) Dursa** m. John Lesnak
(1913-1998) (29 Jun 1907--15 Jan 1974)
m. on 28 Nov 1931 in Youngstown, OH He worked for US Steel, Youngstown. She was a housewife. They lived at 718 Steel St. in Youngstown.
John was born in Youngstown, but in about 1916 moved to Teplička, Slovakia south of Spišská Nová Ves with his parents. He returned to Youngstown in about 1925 without his parents, and lived with an aunt, Anna Megla.
Children:
Margaret Marie (24 Sep 1932, Youngstow–Living).
m. Daniel Robert Toth, (31 Dec 1931 — 06 Mar 2010) on 21 Apr 1956 in Youngstown. He worked as a draftsman. Margie worked as a secretary.

Family Reunion, Youngstown, 1937 at 722 Steel Street.

Very Front: Margie Lesnak; Joanne Pallo.
Front row: Esther Zirbes & Baby Sharon Zirbes; Grandma Mary Dursa; Helen Kostelnik; Vera & Richard Pallo; Jack Conrad.
Back row: Matthew (Dutch) Pallo & "Boots" Pallo; Peter Kostelnik; Susanne Sirilla; Julia Lesnak; Michael Dyuritza (nephew of Grandma).
Third row: Dr. Nick Sopkovich (nephew of Grandma); George Zirbes. Author's archive.

Photos of 6 of the 8 children of Mária Mrozko and Michal Durica

All 8 were born in Poráč, and all of their spouses were born in Poráč. *Author's archive.*

1. *Mária = married Michal Širila, 1890, lived in Lemont, PA, widowed in 1908. Married Michal Ďurša, 1910, moved to Youngstown, OH, widowed in 1934.*
2. *Anna = married Joseph Sopkovich, 1892. Moved to Youngstown, OH*
3. *Katarína (Katka) = married Martin Jurek, Abt 1896. Stayed in Poráč/ Rudňany, Slovakia.*
4. *Eliáš (not shown) (AKA Alec) = married Helen Nemscik, 1900. Moved to Browerville, MN*
5. *Mátej (Matt) (not shown) = married Anna Winsen. Lived in Connellsville, PA*
6. *Ján (John)= married Katharine Varmega, 1905. Had a farm in Herbert, OH, later moved to Youngstown, OH, and later moved to Tuscon, AZ*
7. *Michal (Dorris) = married Anna Fiffick Abt 1913. Lived in Youngstown, OH*
8. *Helena = married Joseph Dursa, 1910. Lived in Uniontown, PA*

(All of these children and their spouses emigrated from Poráč except Katarína.)

Family Group Sheet for Maria Mrozko

Husband: Michal Durica

Birth:	06 Nov 1848 in Porac, (Spis) Slovakia
Death:	04 Nov 1901 in Porac, (Spis) Slovakia
Marriage:	14 Nov 1870 in Porac, (Spis) Slovakia
Father:	Andrej Durica
Mother:	Helena Galajda

Wife: Maria Mrozko

Birth:	11 Mar 1849 in Porac, (Spis) Slovakia
Death:	14 Sep 1913 in Porac, (Spis) Slovakia
Father:	Jan Mrozko
Mother:	Helena Sopkovic

Children:

1 F

Name:	Maria Durica
Birth:	20 Nov 1871 in Porac, (Spis) Slovakia
Death:	03 Jul 1955 in Youngstown, OH, Bur.St. Mary's Byzantine Cemetery.
Marriage:	21 Jul 1890 in Porac, (Spis) Slovakia
Spouse:	Michal* Sirila*

2 F

Name:	Anna Durica
Birth:	19 Dec 1873 in Porac, (Spis) Slovakia
Death:	25 Jan 1950 in Youngstown, OH Bur. St. Mary's Byzantine Cemetery
Marriage:	01 Jul 1892 in Latrobe, PA
Spouse:	Joseph Sopkovich

3 F

Name:	Katarina Durica
Birth:	15 Sep 1876 in Porac, Slovakia
Death:	19 Mar 1947 in Rudnany, Slovakia. Bur. St. Demeter's Greek Catholic Cemetery, Porac
Marriage:	27 May 1896 in Porac, (Spis) Slovakia
Spouse:	Martin Jurek

4 M

Name:	Elias (Eli) Durica (Dyuritza)
Birth:	01 Aug 1879 in Porac, (Spis) Slovakia
Death:	12 Aug 1919 in Star Junction, PA, Bur. St.Stephen's Byz.Cem. Leisenring PA
Marriage:	1900 in Connellsville, Fayette, Pennsylvania, USA
Spouse:	Helena Nemcsik(Nemchik)

5 M

Name:	Matej (Matt) Durica
Birth:	05 Jan 1882 in Porac, (Spis) Slovakia
Death:	11 Nov 1944 in Uniontown, Bur St. Joseph's Cemetery, Uniontown,PA
Spouse:	Anna Winsen

6 M

Name:	Jan (John) Durica
Birth:	23 May 1885 in Porac, (Spis) Slovakia
Death:	09 Jun 1969 in Tuscon, AZ Bur.St.Nicholas Cem.,Campbell,OH
Marriage:	04 Feb 1905 in New Salem, Fayette, Pennsylvania, USA
Spouse:	Katherine Varmega

7 M

Name:	Michal Durica (Dorris)
Birth:	13 Jun 1891 in Porac, (Spis) Slovakia
Death:	15 Jun 1957 in Campbell, OH Bur. Lake Park Mausoleum,Youngstown,OH
Spouse:	Anna Fiffick

8 F

Name:	Helena Durica
Birth:	19 Nov 1893 in Porac, (Spis) Slovakia
Death:	19 Dec 1985 in Uniontown, PA Bur.Hopwood Cemetery, Uniontown,PA
Marriage:	19 Oct 1910 in Fayette County, PA
Spouse:	Joseph Dursa

Family Group Sheet for Jan Mrozko

Husband:		Jan Mrozko
	Birth:	05 Nov 1813 in Porac, (Spis) Slovakia
	Death:	Porac, (Spis) Slovakia
	Marriage:	12 Nov 1835 in Porac, (Spis) Slovakia
	Father:	Matej Mrozko
	Mother:	Maria Szegar

Wife:		Helena Sopkovic
	Birth:	1818 in Porac, (Spis) Slovakia
	Death:	04 May 1860 in Porac, (Spis) Slovakia
	Father:	
	Mother:	

Children:

1 M	Name:	Juraj Mrozko
	Birth:	1843
	Marriage:	09 Mar 1873 in Porac, (Spis) Slovakia
	Spouse:	Katarina Jurek

2 M	Name:	Joannes Mrozko
	Birth:	1847

3 F	Name:	Maria Mrozko ⬅
	Birth:	11 Mar 1849 in Porac, (Spis) Slovakia
	Death:	14 Sep 1913 in Porac, (Spis) Slovakia
	Marriage:	14 Nov 1870 in Porac, (Spis) Slovakia
	Spouse:	Michal Durica

4 M	Name:	Elias Mrozko
	Birth:	1854 in Porac, (Spis) Slovakia
	Death:	16 Jan 1918 in Porac, (Spis) Slovakia
	Spouse:	Catharina Bakos

Family Group Sheet for Andrej Durica

Husband:		Andrej Durica
	Birth:	Porac,Spis, Slovakia
	Death:	Porac,Spis, Slovakia
	Marriage:	08 Feb 1836 in Porac, Spis, Slovakia
	Father:	
	Mother:	

Wife:		Helena Galajda
	Birth:	12 Aug 1816 in Porac, Spis, Slovakia
	Death:	Porac, Spis, Slovakia
	Father:	Jan Galajda
	Mother:	Catharina Petrussny

Children:

1 F	Name:	Anna Durica
	Birth:	09 Sep 1839 in Porac, Spis, Slovakia

2 F	Name:	Catharina Durica
	Birth:	20 Oct 1841 in Porac, Spis, Slovakia

3 F	Name:	Helena Durica
	Birth:	16 Dec 1843 in Porac, Spis, Slovakia

4 M	Name:	Michal Durica ⬅
	Birth:	06 Nov 1848 in Porac,Spis, Slovakia
	Death:	04 Nov 1901 in Porac, Spis, Slovakia
	Marriage:	14 Nov 1870 in Porac,Spis, Slovakia
	Spouse:	Maria Mrozko

5 M	Name:	Matthias Durica
	Birth:	03 Feb 1858 in Porac, Spisska Nova Ves, Slovakia

6 M	Name:	Joannes Durica
	Birth:	29 Aug 1860 in Porac, Spis, Slovakia

Three Ships' Passenger Lists – New York 1820-1957 for Michal Sirila

Mihaly Schirila
in the New York, Passenger Lists, 1820-1957

Name:	Mihaly Schirila
Arrival Date:	10 Jan 1887
Birth Date:	abt 1868
Age:	19
Gender:	Male
Ethnicity/ Nationality:	Hungarian
Place of Origin:	Hungary
Port of Departure:	Bremen, Germany and Southampton, England
Destination:	United States of America
Port of Arrival:	New York, New York
Ship Name:	Eider

Mihaly Serila
in the New York, Passenger Lists, 1820-1957

Name:	Mihaly Serila
Arrival Date:	7 Apr 1891
Birth Date:	abt 1870
Age:	21
Gender:	Female
Ethnicity/ Nationality:	Hungarian
Place of Origin:	Hungary
Port of Departure:	Bremen, Germany and Southampton, England
Destination:	United States of America
Port of Arrival:	New York, New York
Ship Name:	Ems

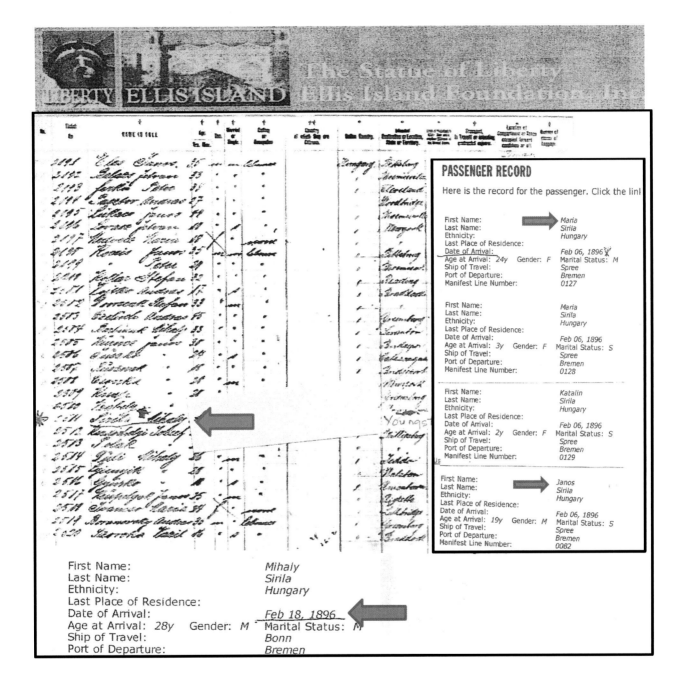

PASSENGER RECORD

Here is the record for the passenger. Click the lin!

First Name: Maria
Last Name: Sirila
Ethnicity: Hungary
Last Place of Residence:
Date of Arrival: Feb 06, 1896
Age at Arrival: 24y Gender: F Marital Status: M
Ship of Travel: Spree
Port of Departure: Bremen
Manifest Line Number: 0127

First Name: Maria
Last Name: Sirila
Ethnicity: Hungary
Last Place of Residence:
Date of Arrival: Feb 06, 1896
Age at Arrival: 3y Gender: F Marital Status: S
Ship of Travel: Spree
Port of Departure: Bremen
Manifest Line Number: 0128

First Name: Katalin
Last Name: Sirila
Ethnicity: Hungary
Last Place of Residence:
Date of Arrival: Feb 06, 1896
Age at Arrival: 2y Gender: F Marital Status: S
Ship of Travel: Spree
Port of Departure: Bremen
Manifest Line Number: 0129

First Name: Janos
Last Name: Sirila
Ethnicity: Hungary
Last Place of Residence:
Date of Arrival: Feb 06, 1896
Age at Arrival: 19y Gender: M Marital Status: S
Ship of Travel: Spree
Port of Departure: Bremen
Manifest Line Number: 0082

First Name: Mihaly
Last Name: Sirila
Ethnicity: Hungary
Last Place of Residence:
Date of Arrival: Feb 18, 1896
Age at Arrival: 28y Gender: M Marital Status: M
Ship of Travel: Bonn
Port of Departure: Bremen

UNITED STATES OF AMERICA

No. 18890

PETITION FOR NATURALIZATION

[Under General Provisions of the Nationality Act of 1940 (Public, No. 853, 76th Cong.)]

To the Honorable the **Common Pleas** Court of **Mahoning County** at **Youngstown Ohio**

This petition for naturalization, hereby made and filed, respectively shows:

(1) My full, true, and correct name is **Mary Dursa (ex Sirila nee Yuritea)**

(2) My present place of residence is **722 Steel St. Youngstown Mahoning Ohio** My occupation is **housewife**

(4) I am **69** years old. (5) I was born on **Dec.25,1871** in **Poracs Hungary**

(6) My personal description is as follows: Sex **female**, color **white** complexion **medium** color of eyes **brown**, color of hair **white** height **5** feet **7** inches, weight **165** pounds, visible distinctive marks **none**, race **Slovak** present nationality **Czechoslovak** (7) I am **widow** married; the name of my wife or husband was **Mihal Dursa** we were married on **July 19,1910**, at **New Salem Penna.**

he or she was born at **Hungary**, on **unknown**

and entered the United States at **unknown** on **unknown** for permanent residence in the United States and now resides at **deceased 10-23-34 at Yo. Ohio**

at _____ ; or became a citizen by _____

(8) I have **9** children; and the name, sex, date and place of birth, and present place of residence of each of said children who is living, are as follows:

Katherine (f) Sept.11,1892 at Poracs Hungary resides Lamont Penna.; Sof (f) Mar.7,1897 at Brownfield Penna resides New York N.Y.; Michael (m) Oct.5,1898 at Vanderbilt Pa. resides New York N.Y.; Joseph (m) March 2 1900 Lamont Pa. resides Yo.Ohio.; Helen (f) July 16,1903 at Lamont Pa. resides Chicago Ill.Justina (f) born March 18,1905 Lamont Pa. resides

(9) My last place of foreign residence was **Poracs Hungary** (10) I emigrated to the United States from **Bremen Germany** (11) My lawful entry for permanent residence in the United States was at **New York N.Y.** under the name of **Maria Sirila** on **Feb. 6, 1896** on the **S.S Spree**

(12) Since my lawful entry for permanent residence I have **not** been absent from the United States, for a period or periods of 6 months or longer, as follows:

DEPARTED FROM THE UNITED STATES			RETURNED TO THE UNITED STATES		
PORT	DATE (Month, day, year)	VESSEL OR OTHER MEANS OF CONVEYANCE	PORT	DATE (Month, day, year)	VESSEL OR OTHER MEANS OF CONVEYANCE

(13) I declared my intention to become a citizen of the United States on **Oct. 7, 1938** in the **Common Pleas**

(14) It is my intention in good faith to become a potentate, State, or sovereignty of whom or which at and have not been for the period of at least 10 years ruction of property, or sabotage; nor a disbeliever in disbelief in or opposition to organized government. ing all of the periods required by law, attached to the ted States. (18) I have resided continuously in the **Feb. 6, 1896**

preceding the date of this petition, to wit, since ralization: No. _____

the _____ (Name of court)

or denial has since been cured or removed. come a citizen of the United States (if such declara- tion Service of my said lawful entry into the United of at least two verifying witnesses required by law.

S.S. SPREE, 1890 North German Lloyd
Courtesy The Peabody Museum of Salem

(21) Wherefore, I, your petitioner for naturalization, pray that I may be admitted a citizen of the United States of America, and that my name be changed to _____

no change

(22) I, aforesaid petitioner, do swear (affirm) that I know the contents of this petition for naturalization subscribed by me, that the same are true to the best of my own knowledge, except as to matters therein stated to be alleged upon information and belief, and that as to those matters I believe them to be true, and that this petition is signed by me with my full, true name: SO HELP ME GOD.

X **mary Dursa**
(Full, true, and correct signature of petitioner, without abbreviation)

c16—19120

Form N-405
(Old 2204 L-B)
U. S. DEPARTMENT OF JUSTICE
IMMIGRATION AND NATURALIZATION SERVICE
(Edition of 1-13-41)

(left margin, sideways) Chicago, Illinois; s Susana (f) Dec. 14, 1907 at Lamont Pa. resides Yo.Ohio; Julia (f) April 13, York; Vera (f) May 28, 1911 Lamont Pa. resides Yo.Ohio; 1913, Vanderbilt Pa. resides Youngstown Ohio

COUSINS

FAMILIES

COUSINS (*Author's archive.*)

1   Joann Pallo Klacik
2. Sharon Zirbes Fuller (author)
3. Margie Lesnak Toth
4. Georgette Zirbes
5. Richard Pallo
6. Margaret Kuchta Cleary + spouse
7. Esther Sirilla Hickey
8. George Sirilla + spouse
9. June Shrilla Carducci + spouse
10. Richard Shrilla + spouse
11. Richard Shrilla + Margie Lesnak Toth
12. Bette Kuchta Blick + spouse
13. Dorothy Sopkovich Pohmurski + author
14. Štefan Cvengroš + author
15. František Cvengroš + author
16. Demeter Širila + author
17. Helen Conrad Licastro + spouse
18. Maureen Steffen Peel + Family
19. Shirley Cave Navarro
20. Petrosky (Novak) siblings: Joe, Antoinette, John

FAMILIES (Courtesy of relatives' archives.)
1. 1926, Uniontown, PA Family of **Helen Durica Dursa** (sister of Maria Durica) + husband Joseph
    Dursa. Children: Anna (b. 1916); Joseph (b. 1918); Frank (b. 1923); Margaret (b. 1921); John (b.
    1912) (*Š.Cvengroš archive.*)
2. 1932, Youngstown, OH Family of **Anna Durica Sopkovich** (sister of Maria Durica) (husband
    Joseph Sopkovich deceased.
    Children: Michael (b. 1899); Mary (b. 1893); Dr. Nickolas (b. 1909); mother Anna; Steve (b.
    1895).   (*D.Pohmurski archive.*)
3. 2013, Laguna Niguel, CA Maureen Duritza Steffen Peel + brother + grandchildren and great
    grandchildren of **John Duritza**, (brother of Maria Durica). (*M.Peel archive.*)
4. 1930, Uniontown, PA Family of **Katharine Sirilla Duritsa** (daughter of Maria Durica Sirilla) + John
    Duritsa. Back row: father John; George (b.1910); mother Katie; John (b.1912); Ann (b.1914);
    Front row: Nicholas (b.1920); Helen (b.1922). (*S. Navarro archive.*)
5. Abt 1949, Youngstown, OH Family of **Joseph Shrilla** (son of Maria Durica Sirilla)
    Children: June (b. 1928); Richard (b. 1931). (*Author's archive.*)
6. 1950, Tinley Park, IL Family of **Esther Justine Sirilla Zirbes** (daughter of Maria Durica Sirilla)
    Children: Georgette (b. 1940); Sharon (b. 1936). *Author's archive.*)
7. 2000, Youngstown, OH   Grandchildren of **Vera Dursa Pallo** (center) (daughter of Maria Durica
    Sirilla Dursa). *(Pallo archive.)*

Churches cited in this memoir:

Sv. Demetrius Grécko-Katolícka Kostol,
Founded in 1640
Poráč, Slovakia
Father Milan Gabor
Demetrius@iarelative.com

St. Stephen's Byzantine Catholic Church,
Founded in 1892
P.O. Box 128 (3120 West Crawford Avenue)
Leisenring, PA 15455
Father Ronald Larko   Tel. 724-628-6611

St. John the Baptist Byzantine Catholic Church,
Founded in 1911
185 East Main Street
Uniontown, PA 15401 Tel. 724-438-6027

St. Nicholas Byzantine Catholic Church,
Founded in 1911
504 S. Liberty Street
Perryopolis, PA 15473 Tel. 724-736-4344

St. Mary's Byzantine Catholic Church,
Founded in 1900, located on Steel St.,
Youngstown, OH
New church founded in 1956 at
356 South Belle Vista Avenue
Youngstown, OH 44509 Tel. 330-799-8163
www.saintmarysbyz.com

St. Nicholas Byzantine Catholic Church,
Founded in 1919
1898 Wilson Avenue
Youngstown, OH (Struthers) 44506
Tel. 330-743-0419
Stnick9000@aol.com

Marriage Ceremony at St. Demeter's Church
Poráč of Mária Širillová and Josef Polkabla, 1985.
Author's photo.

St. Nicholas from the cover of the prayer book of Esther
Sirilla, August 8, 1923, Star Junction, PA
Author's archive.

Timeline of Slovak History – Maps

The Austro-Hungarian Empire, 1867-1914

From "With Their Backs to the Mountains", 2015 by Paul Robert Magocsi, p. 130.
Permission from the author.

Czechoslovakia, 1918-1992

A-Z Maps online.

Maps:

Independent Slovakia & Its Neighbors since January 1, 1993.

A-Z Maps online.

Village of Poráč & neighboring villages.

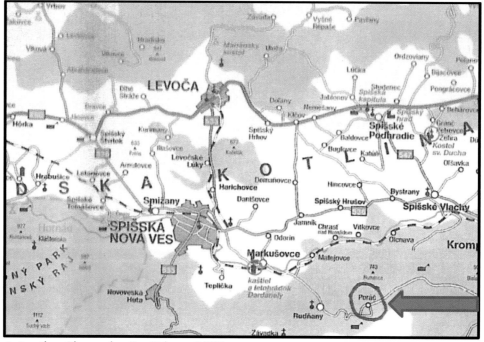

Autoatlas Slovenska, Bratislava, 2003.

TIMELINE OF SLOVAK HISTORY

Part I – 400s-1800s:

400s-500s Slavic people arrive in Central Europe from the Pripet Marshes and plains between the Baltic and Black Seas.

600s Samo's empire, the first political unit of Slavs.

700s Principality of Nitra, with Prince Pribina as ruler.

800s Great Moravian Empire with Prince Rastislav as ruler.

863 Cyril & Methodius, missionaries from Thessoloniki, at the request of Rastislav, arrive in Great Moravian Empire from Constantinople with a new alphabet of the Slavic language and a translation of the Bible in Old Slavonic. The new alphabet was called Glagolitic, later named Cyrillic, after its creator.

896 Hungarian Conquest, led by Magyar Chief Árpád, defeats Prince Svätopluk and lays claim to the Danube Basin.

955 End of the Magyar pillaging of Europe by the Defeat of the Magyars in Augsburg.

1000 Rule of Hungarian King Stephen, (975-1038) forming the political kingdom of Greater Hungary, subjugating the Slovaks along the Tatra Mountains and referring to the Slovak region as Felvidék, the Highlands.

1526 Turkish defeat of Magyars at Mohač. Beginning of the Hapsburg Dynasty.

1843 Publication of Ľudivít Štur's codification of the Slovak language based on central Slovak dialect.

1848 Political revolutions in Europe. Slavic Congress in Prague and the beginning of Slovak nationalism.

1867 Duel monarchy established between Austria-Hungary; Slovaks become part of the Kingdom of Hungary with severe suppression of Slovak language and Slovak cultural institutions.

1890s Beginning of serious emigration of Slovaks, mostly to United States.

Part II 1900s

1918 End of WWI. Hapsburg-ruled empire collapses and Czechs and Slovaks together form Czechoslovakia. Tomáš Garrigue Masaryk becomes the first president.

1939 Germany occupies the Czech region as a German "protectorate"; the Slovak region becomes an independent state under Nazi German administration.

1944 Slovak National Uprising occurs in central Slovakia, with Slovak troops, partisans, Soviets, and some OSS Americans and British rising up against the Nazis. The uprising is defeated by the Germans.

1945 End of WWII. Soviet army liberates Slovakia and Czechoslovakia state is restored by the Allies.

1948 Communist party takes control of Slovak politics.

1968 "Prague Spring" creates a relaxation of politics through leadership of Alexander Dubček, a Slovak.

1989 Velvet Revolution overthrows the Communist Party rule of 42 years. Vaclav Havel elected president of Czechoslovakia with political reforms in process.

1992 Slovakia's government declares independence from Czechoslovakia and the new Republic of Slovakia is official on January 1, 1993.

Part III 2000s

2004 Slovakia joins NATO and the EU.

2005 Slovakia approves a "flat tax" which encourages foreign investments, ie: KIA, VW, Ford, US Steel.

2009 Slovakia adopts the Euro currency. Hockey is still Slovakia's #1 sport.

2015 Central and western Slovakia experiences economic growth with foreign investors.

2018 Prime Minister: Peter Pellegrini

2019 President: Zuzana Caputova (As of April 1, 2019.)

Within Poráč

Left to right: St. Demetrius Church; Anička Širillová's First Communion, age 9; Folklórna Skupina, (mixed chorus of Poráč); Author in folk dress (kroj) 1985; Church and "old town."
Author's archive.

History of the Village of Poráč

Cover from Š. Hanuščin's book, Poráč.

Located in the northeastern part of Slovakia is the county of Spiš, and in this county hidden high up in the mountains is the village called Poráč, where historically the occupants were primarily farmers and miners of copper ore, iron ore, mercury ore.

Poráč has had several names:
1382 = Vereshegy (pronounced Vereshhedge) in Hungarian meaning Red Hill.
1471 = Rotenberg meaning Red Hill in German
1773 = Poracz, Palocz, Polish spelling for Poráč
1808 = Poráč (pronounced Porach) in Slovak

Population statistics:
1787 = Hungarian census 1,017
1869 = Hungarian census 1,436
1900 = 1,800
1920 = 880
1970 = 1,006
2011 = approx. 1,200

Spišský hrad. Author's photo.

History of Settlement:
In 1277 the first record of the village appears, and this was after the 1241 plundering of the Tatars in Central Europe. Despite the defensive advantage of Spiš Castle (about 20 km northeast of Poráč) and the largest castle ruins in Central Europe, the Tatars were able to invade as far as the town of Levoča, and it is believed that many Slovaks fled from this area into the canyons of the Slovak Ore Mountains. Poráč is at the end of one of these canyons. The village lies on a ridge between the Poráč and Gold Creeks, and the larger mountains rich in minerals rise to the east. Forests of spruce, hemlock and fir and rich pastures for sheep and cows surround the village. Spiš Castle can be seen to the northeast, and the High Tatra Mountains can be seen to the northwest.

In the 1300s the village emerged as a mining settlement and sheep herding area. Some historians believe that Lemko Rusyn shepherds from the Galicia area (now Poland) came from the villages of Čarna Voda, Bila Voda, Šljachtova, Javirký, all near today's Nowy Targ, at the request of the Hungarian Count Mariássy, who owned the Markušovce Castle and the nearby villages of Koterbach and Poráč. Other villages nearby (Zavadka and Teplička) were also settled by these same Rusyn-Lemko (gorale) shepherds. It is also believed that these shepherds were originally Vlachs who migrated north from today's Romania, in an attempt to escape the Tatar's attacks. (It is interesting to note that a few km. east of Poráč is the village of Spišské Vlachy.)

Germans were also colonizers in the Spiš area after the Tatar invasions. Miners, farmers, foresters and craftsmen were recruited from the areas of Holland, Flanders, Rhine-Mosel, Thuringia and Saxony. Most of these Germans were originally headed for Transylvania, but some stopped and settled in the Spiš area. By 1247, 24 towns in the Spiš area existed with German settlers, Poráč being one. It is recorded that in 1593 Poráč had an elementary school that was German Lutheran. After the Catholic Counter Reformation, the villagers returned to the Greek Orthodox faith and made St. Demetrius the village patron, naming their church after him. It is usually accepted that until 1918, Poráč was grouped as a Rusyn village because of the particular language dialect practiced and the Greek Catholic religion, which is the norm for Rusyn villages. After the formation of Czechoslovakia as a state, most people of Poráč called themselves Slovaks; the émigré's from Spiš to the US also called themselves Slovaks. However, the term "Rusnák" is still heard in reference to people living in Poráč today, and many descendants in the US today call themselves Rusyn.

Here is a list of some of the common surnames found **today** in Poráč, according to the author Štefan Hanuščin in his book **Poráč**, published in 2003, (not yet completely translated into English from the Slovak):

Bakoš, Barbuš, Belej, Bilpuch, Bodnovič, Cebul'a, <u>Ďurica</u>, <u>Ďurša</u>, Fiffik, Hardon, Harviščak, Hanučšin, Kinik, Kolesár, Korchnak, Liška, Lorenc, Macala, Midlik, Počatko, Polkabla, Sivačko, Stanislav, <u>Širila</u>, Vrábel Vansač, Volčko, Vojtila, Zavačan.

The emigration period from 1890-1920 from Poráč shows that the village decreased by 50%, but the emigrés created a new "Poráč home" primarily in Fayette County of western Pennsylvania and later into suburban Campbell near Youngstown, Ohio. The cemetery of St. Stephens Greek Catholic Church in Leisenring, Pennsylvania is a showcase of Poráčane burials. Most of the above family surnames are still seen in Poráč today. It is not an understatement to say that if you knocked at every house in Poráč today and asked if the family lost any relatives to the great emigration, almost every house would answer that they knew of at least one family member who left, and in most cases more than one member. What we know is that the emigrés, for the most part, stuck together and created their own communities; their life centered around the church, most within the Greek Catholic Church (called Byzantine Rite today). They emphasized a strong Americanization of their descendants. The 3rd, 4th, and 5th generation descendants have either been totally assimilated or there are those who have a growing awareness and interest in knowing more about their roots and their ancestral village. It is never too late to begin to strengthen these ties. This book is dedicated to all of those who live around the world who may have or will have returned to their ancestral town.

Internet search sites:
www.iarelative.com/porac/index.html
www.rusynsofpa.blogspot.com % Richard D. Custer
Obečný urad, Poráč 61, Poráč, Slovakia
obecporac@demax.sk

Uncle Mike Sirilla & Sharon, 1984.
Author's archive.

HISTORY OF EASTERN EUROPEAN CATHOLICS: THE GREEK CATHOLIC CHURCH

There are three main churches sited in this memoir of Maria Dursa:

    Sväty Demetrius Grécko-katolícka Kostol, Poráč, Slovakia

        (St. Demetrius Greek Catholic Church, Poráč, Slovakia)

    St. Stephen's Greek Catholic Church, Leisenring, Pennsylvania

    St. Mary's Greek Catholic Church, Youngstown, Ohio

Therefore a necessary explanation of the history of the Greek Catholic Church is needed.

The year 863 marks the year when the missionaries Cyril and his brother Methodius converted the Slavs in the area of today's Nitra, Slovakia to Christianity. Before making the travel to central Europe, Cyril, in his hometown of Thessaloniki, Greece, codified the Slavic language basing the new alphabet on the Greek symbols and used this alphabet to translate the Bible into the Slavic language. This Bible was used in the conversion of the Slavs and provided the basis for the new "Slavic Christianity."

The area of central Europe was later overrun by Roman Catholics (the Latin rite) from western Europe, a political move.

Eastern Europe developed into the Byzantine rite, commonly called Orthodox. In the 17th century, when the Orthodox clergy found pressure from Roman Catholicism from the occupying Hungarians in what is today eastern Slovakia and western Ukraine, and seeing the advantages that the training of priests could benefit from under Rome, 63 orthodox priests met in 1646 in the city of Užhorod (a small city on the border of today's Slovakia and Ukraine) and accepted the authority of <u>Rome</u>, with the following exceptions:

    I. priests would continue to be allowed to marry

    2 the use of icons and iconostasis would remain

    3. communion would continue to use both bread and wine

    4. baptism and confirmation would continue to be simultaneous at birth

    5. use of Old Slavonic (not Latin) would continue in the liturgy

    6. there would still be more singing in the mass, with less use of organ music

    7. the Julian calendar, not the Gregorian calendar, would be retained

    8. the sensuality of the Byzantine rite and meeting God with the heart would be retained icons=_sight_; singing=_hearing_; kissing icons=_touch_; communion of bread & wine=_taste_ incense=_smell_

After this agreement, **The Union of Užhorod**, the church called itself the Uniate Church, but later found that name ineffective and changed the name to "Greek Catholic," "Greek" being synonymous with "Byzantine" or "eastern" to differentiate it from "Roman Catholic."

Today, churches in the US like St. Stephen's in Leisenring or St. Mary's in Youngstown call themselves St. Stephen's Byzantine Rite Catholic Church and St. Mary's Byzantine Rite Catholic Church to indicate the influence of the Eastern rite. The continuation of the use of "Greek" was confusing according to the officialdom of Rome.

Today there is more use of the local language in the mass as seen In the use of English in the US and the use of Slovak in Slovak churches. (However, Slovak churches continue to use the "Greek Catholic" name.)   Also in the US there is more regulation for priests NOT to marry.   Many of the historic Greek Catholic churches in the US have been forced to assimilate as Russian Orthodox today, and many of these churches were originally founded by Slovak or Rusyn immigrants. Some parishioners believe that the conversion from Greek Catholic to Orthodox was due to the permission that Orthodox priests in the US could marry.

Sources:

Byzantine Catholic Church in Slovakia by Andrej Skoviera (www.grkat.nfo.sk/eng/intro2.html)
Encyclopedia of Rusyn History and Culture by Paul Magocsi (pp. 480-482)
The Rusyns of Slovakia by Paul Magocsi (pp.17-22)

Footnote on the use of "Rusyn":

Despite many Slovak historians' documentation, (based on existence of the Greek Catholic Church and on the dialect of the village) that the village of **Poráč** (about which this memoir is rooted) is of **Rusyn** heritage, (and this village is still referred to by nearby villagers as "Rusnak"), today's residents of Poráč call themselves Slovak because standard Slovak is the official language of the country and standard Slovak is the language of instruction in the schools. No doubt there is use of the local Rusyn dialect in the home and on the streets and alleys of Poráč.

St. Nicholas Greek Catholic Church in Bodružal. This church was built in 1658 and is the oldest wooden church in Slovakia. Today It is designated a UNESCO historical monument. It is located near the town of Svidnik in eastern Slovakia. Author's photo.

These wooden Greek Catholic churches are scattered over the area of eastern Slovakia, on an east-west axis, the altar facing east. The construction is in three parts: the sanctuary, the nave, and the choir, back, middle, front respectively. The <u>entrance</u> is in the highest part, the choir. Each section is topped with its own cupola, then topped with a three piece cross. (It is a miracle that these churches survived the devastation of WWII.) The construction is entirely of wood, including the nails. The outside is covered with fir shingles, and the church is usually set a short distance from the village, usually surrounded by fir trees. The weathering is natural, so the overall look is brown, somber, and rustic.

SLOVAK LANGUAGE PRONUNCIATION GUIDE and

Guide to Slovak Surnames in Poráč and USA

Pronunciation of Vowels:	Pronunciation of Consonants:	The Stress on any word falls on the
a as in shut	c as in sits	**first** syllable. Examples:
á as in father	č as in chew	Mária = Mahreea Elíáš = Eleeahsh
e as in met	ch as in Loch	Poráč = Porach
é as in air	j as in yellow	dobrý deň = dobree dyenj
i,y as in pit	n as in not	The curly accent mark over consonants
í,ýas in see	ň as in onion	is called "háčik" meaning "hook"in English
o as in pot	ř as in rz	
ó as in poor	s as in hiss	
	š as in posh	
	z as in zebra	
	ž as in pleasure	

Current common Family Surnames in Poráč
 from Štefan Hanuščin's book *Poráč:*

Variation of spellings found in American documents of family surnames used in this memoir:

Bakoš

Barbuš

Belej

Bilpuch

Bodnovič

Cebula

**Ďurica

**Ďurša

Fifik

Hardoň

Harviščak

Hanuščin

Kinik

Kolesár

Korchňak

Liška

Lorenc

Macala

Mydlik

Počatko

Polkabla

Sivačko

Stanislav

**Širila

Vrábel

Vansač

Volčko

Vojtila

For Širila: Sirilla, Shirilla, Schirilla, Sherella, Shrilla

For Ďurica: Duricza, Duritsa, Duritza, Dyuritza, Gyuricza

For Ďurša: Dursa, Djursa, Doorsa, Gyursa, Dorris

THE SPIŠ DIALECT (Spišské nárečie)
Mária's four letters were written in the Spiš dialect, being the most western province of eastern Slovakia. This area was influenced by Germans (Zips in German) and Hungarians (Szepes in Magyar). IE: In Spiš dialect the word for roof is "**dach**" the same as in German. The Standard Slovak for roof is *strecha*. The Spiš word for breakfast is "**frištik**"; in German "frühstuck." Some sounds are also softer in the Spiš dialect: In regular Slovak the word for man, *chlap,* becomes "**hlop**", just like the Slovak word for bread, *chlieb,* becomes" **hleb**."

Softer sounds are also heard In Spiš, when "s" softens to "š". IE: Instead of the Slovak for "sit down" *sadni si,* in Spiš it is "**šedni ši.**" D's also soften in Spiš. IE: In Slovak "grandfather"*dedo* becomes "**dzedo**" in Spiš.
The influence of the Rusyn dialect on Poráč and other Rusyn villages in Spiš is also significant .

American Slovak Michael Sirilla, center, Poráč, Slovakia. 1984. Author's photo.

As you can see by the photo, Mike is enjoying an afternoon conversation with the local *"Babičkas"* (Grannies). He can communicate with them in his "Old Spiš dialect" that he learned from his mother, Mária, who was born in Poráč. The women understood him perfectly, although sometimes laughing at his use of outdated words. This was his hobby in retirement and widowhood: spending two weeks every summer in August in Poráč.

Four Slovak Women – Poráč
Left to right:
Alena Polkablová Piaková, b. 1986
Mária Širillová Polkablová, b. 1963
Mária Fabianová Širillová, b. 1939
Timea Piaková, b. 2011
Author's photo.

These women are from the family of Demeter Širila (1938-2010) who was second cousin to the author.

NUT ROLLS (orechovník) and/or POPPY SEED ROLLS (mákovník)

This recipe makes 2 rolls:
1 package active dry yeast
¼ cup warm milk
½ cup sugar
3/4 cup butter
½ cup milk, heated to lukewarm
3 cups flour
½ teas. salt
1 whole egg

Dissolve some sugar in ¼ cup warm milk. Crumble the dry yeast in this mixture. Let stand for 8-10 minutes. Beat egg and sugar. Heat rest of milk to lukewarm.   Melt butter in lukewarm milk. Combine all of the above mixtures, including salt, in large bowl.

Add flour little by little and mix well. Turn dough out onto a floured board and knead until smooth and elastic. (Knead for 5-10 minutes.) Cover with a towel and let stand in a warm place until it rises. Punch down and cover again until it rises. It takes about 2 hours to rise.   Punch down and divide into 2 equal portions. With a floured rolling pin, roll out 1 portion into a rectangle, relatively thin. Spread filling on the surface and roll up jelly-roll fashion, tucking in the ends. Place on baking sheet, top side down. Repeat with remaining dough and place on baking sheet.   Brush top of each roll with a mixture of a beaten whole egg and milk and prick rolls in a few places with a fork. Let stand for 20-30 minutes. Place rolls top side down in a 350 degree oven for 30-45 minutes, checking   regularly so that the bottoms of the rolls do not burn. Let cool. To serve, cut into slices about 1 inch thick.   *Author's recipe.*

FILLINGS:
Walnut:
1 cup sugar
2 cups ground walnuts
1 tablespoon lemon grind
1 ½ teaspoons ground cinnamon
Optional:
¼ cup raisins,
2 tablespoons apricot jam
Egg whites
dash of rum

Poppy Seed:
1 can Solo poppy seed filling
1 teaspoon grated lemon grind
1 teaspoon vanilla extract
Optional:
¾ cup raisins, or dash of rum
Milk to ease the thickness

Author's cross stitch, 2001.
"Without work, there are no cakes." or
"No pain, no gain."

SUGGESTED READINGS:

Non Fiction:

Alzo, Lisa A, *The Polish, Czech, and Slovak Genealogy Guide.* Blue Ash, OH: Family Tree Books, 2016.
   Finding Your Slovak Ancestors. Baltimore, MD: Gateway Press, 2008.
   Three Slovak Women. Toronto, Canada: Heritage Productions, 2005.

Edwards, Brendan. *Slovakia, the Essential Guide to Customs and Culture.* London: Kuperard Ltd, 2011.

Ekoniak, Loretta A. and Susan J. Sumers. *The Slovaks of Greater Mahoning Valley.* Charleston, SC: Arcadia Publishing, 2011.

Hanuscin, Štefan. *Poráč* (In Slovak). Spišská Nová Ves, Slovakia: Proff, 2003.

Hovanec, Evelyn A. *Common Lives of Uncommon Strength: the Women of the Coal and Coke Era of Southwestern Pennsylvania 1880-1970.* Uniontown, PA: Stefano's Printing, 2001.

Jason, Sonya N. *Maria Gulovich: OSS Heroine of World War II.* Jefferson, NC: McFarland, 2009.

Kirschbaum, Stanislav J. *A History of Slovakia: The Struggle for Survival.* New York: Palgrave, 2006.

Lockwood, Jason. *Banana Peels on the Tracks: Coming of Age in Post-Communist Slovakia.* Bloomwood Media Publication (self published), 2015.

Magocsi, Paul Robert. *The Rusyns of Slovakia: An Historical Survey.* New York: Columbia U. Press, 1993.

Palka, John. *My Slovakia, My Family. One Family's role in the Birth of a Nation.* Minneapolis, MN: Kirk House Publishers, 2012.

Palovic, Zusana and Gabriela Bereghazyova. *Slovakia: the Legend of the Linden.* Bratislava, SK: Global Slovakia, 2018.

Fiction:

Bell, Thomas. *Out of This Furnace.* Pittsburgh: U. of Pittsburgh Press, 1941.

Jason, Sonya. *Icon of Spring.* Middleton, PA: Jednota Press, 1987.

Karas, Nicholas Stevenson. *Hunky: The Immigrant Experience.* Bloomington IN: First Books, 2005.

Krivak, Andrew. *The Sojourn.* New York: Bellevue Literary Press, 2011.

Morris, Heather. *The Tattooist of Auschwitz: a novel, based on the true story of love and survival.* Main characters are from Krombachy and Vranov Nad Topl'ou, Slovakia. NY: Harper Collins, 2018.

Parobek, Ginnka. *Vagabonds in Cleveland.* Cleveland, OH: Create Space Independent Publishing, 2013.

Tierney, Colleen B. *The Weight of Coal & Lace: The Story of Andras and Sophie Kuchta.* Self published: 2012. (The author is a great granddaughter of this memoir's subject: Mary Dursa.)

About the Author, Sharon Zirbes Fuller

I was born in Chicago, and in 1941 I moved with my family to Tinley Park, IL where I spent my childhood and teenage years. After graduating from the U. of Illinois in 1958 I taught high school English and discovered "the West," and I especially fell in love with Colorado and the Rocky Mountains. It was later that I saw a slide show about Slovakia, and I was shocked to see the similarities of geography between the land near the Tatra Mountains and the land within the Rocky Mountains. That began my love affair with Slovakia and the ancestral home of my mother's family in the village of Poráč in the province of Spiš.

I have visited the village and relatives 11 times, and even though I do not speak Slovak language very well and know just some of the history and culture of the Slovaks, I feel such comfort in hearing the language and feasting on the beauty of the scenery; I feel there like **I am Home.**

This memoir was about 50 years in my mind and some 5 years in the making. I hope it inspires readers to visit their ancestral village wherever it is and hopefully to write their own memoir of their family's history of immigration.

There is no past which can be brought back. There is only an eternally new time, building on the extended elements of the past. And the genuine longing must always be to be productive, to create something new and better.
Johann Wolfgang von Goethe

Author's cross stitch, 2008. *Slovenská bohyňa s vták* (Slovak Goddess with bird).
From Mary B. Kelly's booklet *Embroidering The Goddesses of Slovakia,*
Denver, CO, Counted Thread Press, 1995.

Index

Made in the USA
Middletown, DE
12 June 2021